Navigating Money Markets & Men

A Modern Woman's guide to financial independence

Navigating Money, Markets & Men © 2024 Judy Williams

All Rights Reserved. No part of this book may be reproduced in any form or by any electronic or mechanical means including information storage and retrieval systems, without permission in writing from the author. The only exception is by a reviewer, who may quote short excerpts in a review.

This is a work of non-fiction. The events and conversations in this book have been set down to the best of the author's ability, although some names and details may have been changed to protect the privacy of individuals. Every effort has been made to trace or contact all copyright holders. The publishers will be pleased to make good any omissions or rectify any mistakes brought to their attention at the earliest opportunity.

Printed in Australia

Cover and internal design by Shawline Publishing Group Pty Ltd

Images in this book are copyright approved for Shawline Publishing Group Pty Ltd

First printing: August 2024

Shawline Publishing Group Pty Ltd

www.shawlinepublishing.com.au

Paperback ISBN 978-1-9231-7203-6

eBook ISBN 978-1-9231-7214-2

Hardback ISBN 978-1-9231-7225-8

Distributed by Shawline Distribution and Lightning Source Global

Shawline Publishing Group acknowledges the traditional owners of the land and pays respects to the Elders, past, present and future.

 A catalogue record for this work is available from the National Library of Australia

Judy Williams

Navigating Money Markets & Men

A Modern Woman's guide to financial independence

For the boys and their beautiful families.

Author's note

There is a great deal to know about managing money successfully; this is just a start. It's become apparent that we forgot to share much of this knowledge with our kids, especially the girls.

Girls are particularly vulnerable because they are generally paid less, face discrimination in the marketplace and may take career breaks to have children, meaning less superannuation. Difficult partners can financially abuse them or they may just feel they don't have the knowledge to choose their own path. It is more important than ever that girls be given the tools to be financially independent.

This is that toolkit.

I was always good with money, but things went haywire when I married my husband. Thus followed two decades of financial chaos before I finally separated my financial affairs from his and eventually moved on.

This book tells the story of how to do it for yourself, what to watch for and how to buy things, from cars to houses. Woven into the information are the stories of the situations I faced and how they were overcome.

Financial resilience empowers women and, in turn, their children. It's a better result for everyone. But this book goes beyond that. Once the money is sorted, how do you find your perfect job and develop into the woman you dream of being?

This is hard-won knowledge being passed on for the benefit of the girls that follow because when women do well, society does well.

Judy Williams

Foreword

Financial meltdown

Imagine a world where you can work less and focus on your hobbies or personal goals with enough money to see you through to your inevitable end. Through financial resilience, independence and empowerment, this is a goal that you can achieve. Things are good for me now, but that wasn't always the case.

I remember it so clearly – the day I decided I finally had to take control of my family's finances. I was in my late forties, married for about seventeen years and had two preteen boys.

My husband and I were renting a house in an expensive part of Sydney, Australia, and we had started a business together that did well initially but, in its fourth year, was foundering. Knowing the company was a sinking ship, I got a job as a property manager in a real estate office, where my primary role was ensuring landlords got their rent.

That fateful day, I was at my desk and the door to the storefront office blew open. It banged against the wall. Two people marched in, waving papers and looking at me through the Perspex office wall dividers. They stomped into the manager's office, threw down papers, had a heated discussion and then walked out. My manager relayed that my wages would be garnished for lack of payment of rent. That meant my employer was required to pay my debtor before he paid me. I was allowed a tiny amount of my wage to live on.

It was a humiliating day because my job at the company was to collect rent for landlords, and unbeknownst to me, we hadn't been paying our rent. I knew nothing about it; I thought my husband was paying the rent from our joint account, but he had been spending it elsewhere.

This was catastrophic. It was close to Christmas, my husband was out of work and we had no other income. After I got over the shock of the office intrusion, I walked across the street to a bank, opened an account in my name and immediately got to work separating my financial affairs from his. This not only empowered me in a difficult situation, but it also saved my (economic) life down the track.

One day, you, too, will face your financial doomsday. It might be the loss of a job, it might be a marriage breakdown, it might be having to care for someone close to you with an illness or it might even be the death of a partner. All these things can be devastating financially but you can recover if you know how to prepare for it and address it. Building financial resilience is crucial to surviving and living your best possible life.

Dr Barbara O'Neill defines financial resilience as 'the ability to withstand life events that impact one's income and assets'. People build economic resilience by having resources and plans in place so they can recover from anything life throws at them. To be financially resilient, you must know how to manage your money carefully.

While the information in this book can be applied by both men and women, I'm focused on women specifically because there is still an element of the Princess complex when we raise girls. The idea is that someone will sweep them off their feet and take care of them. That's not the outcome that's happening for many women. Aside from the excessive pressure it puts on our young men to provide, some women still think that knowing or understanding money is somehow grubby or not their place.

Money is a form of power. You don't need a lot of it, but you need enough, and by learning to manage it, you have control and choices. This book is about passing on all that I have learned so you will recognise gaps in your financial affairs and set to work fixing them before your financial meltdown catches up with you. When you protect yourself and increase your economic resiliency by building better money habits, you'll be able to focus more on the things that bring you fulfilment and joy.

There is a motivational theory called Maslow's Hierarchy of Human Needs. Maslow uses a pyramid metaphor to describe the different levels of human needs that lead to happiness. The pyramid's base represents your basic needs: food, warmth and shelter. These needs must be met to move on to the next level representing your psychological needs: belonging, love and esteem. Only after meeting your psychological needs can you work on your self-fulfilment needs: creativity and self-actualisation.

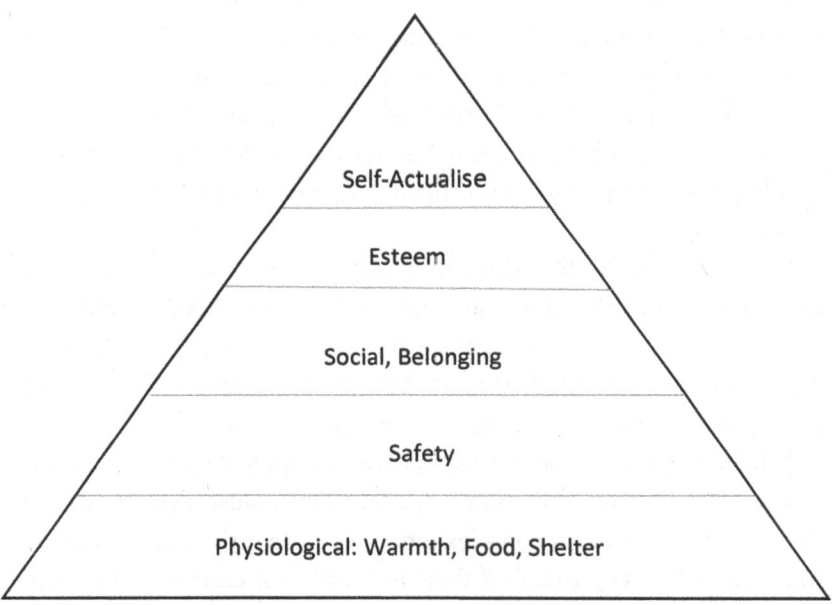

You will often bounce around on this hierarchy. When you suffer a financial setback, you are back to the base, sorting out your basic needs, and the higher activities are ignored for the time being. The faster you can resolve the lower, basic needs, the quicker you can return to your higher self-fulfilment needs.

Unfortunately, too many women are so busy resolving their basic needs that they don't have time for the higher needs. The lack of security in our fundamental needs (housing, food, job security) devastates our personal development. Compound that with a hysterical push towards consumerism and competitiveness on social media that shows everyone having a better life than you, and we are surprised that we are facing a massive mental health crisis!

Nowhere in the hierarchy of needs is money mentioned. But of course, to live, we all need some income to pay for what we need and want. The wiser we are with our money, the more likely we will move past the basic needs level of the pyramid to pursue meeting our psychological and self-actualisation needs.

How you make and use money is the root of your future financial independence and subsequent self-actualisation and happiness. This book will first look at how to build better money habits to meet your essential physical needs. We'll then look at how to buy better to improve your preparation for the worst. Finally, we'll look at what it means to invest in yourself and your happiness once you've achieved financial stability and empowerment.

Along the way, I'll show you what I have learned about saving, managing and growing my funds. I'm now a woman in my sixties, and I am comfortable even though I have overcome significant financial adversity several times in my life. It can take months or, more usually, several years to achieve all that I am about to cover. But it is worth it. Wherever you are on your financial journey, it's not too late. You can always take steps to become more financially independent and resilient.

Part 1

BUILD BETTER MONEY HABITS

Chapter 1

A new way to think about spending

Exchanging time for money

Let's start with your relationship with money.

We are all born with a set amount of time on the planet to realise our potential. We don't know how much time. That is one of life's great mysteries. We blunder along, thinking we have lots of time. This is our default position.

When we start to become aware of money, we become consumers. We want things. They are put in front of us. They are sold in bright colours with happy jingles and we are taught to desire. We didn't want these things before they were presented to us. They were sold to us. The desire was created out of nothing. This is marketing.

Our exposure to marketing starts at a very young age and becomes more pervasive the older we get.

So, we decide we need money to buy the things we want. To get money, we need to work.

We are born with time. This is all we have, and we don't know how much of it we will have. But when we work, we willingly trade our time for money.

This is explored in a book called *Your Money or Your Life* by Vicki Robin and Joe Dominguez. They outline a stepped process for becoming financially independent.

Their first step is determining how much money you have made in your lifetime. This is a brain-bending exercise that takes quite a bit of time.

This hurts because once you add all that up, the second stage is to look around you and see what you exchanged your life essence for. Their point is that if you are exchanging your life (time and energy) for money, it better be worth it. And they're right!

They take it a step further, and this part of the equation hurts. What are you actually earning when you exchange your time for money? I will keep the math simple here for illustration purposes.

Let's say you make a figure of $1000 a week gross. That translates to $25 per hour in a 40-hour week. But that's not really what you are getting. First, your employer will probably take out a sum of money for taxes, holiday pay, sick leave, etc. (if you are lucky enough to get it).

That leaves you roughly $800 per week. Then if you add in the commute (let's say two hours per day), that brings your hourly rate down to $16 because that is 10 hours a week that are not yours to do with as you please. What does it cost you for your commute? Petrol? Car? Transit? Insurance? Take it off. Then clothes and shoes. Then maybe daycare costs. You're down to not very much per hour.

Once you have calculated the actual exchange that you are making per hour of your work, whatever it is, you will be at a much lower rate of pay than you initially thought you were making. Don't despair.

This is an integral part of the brain shift that must happen.

If you work out that you are trading your life essence (time) for about $10 an hour (if you are lucky), are you going to squander a nearly full week's worth of work/hours on a pair of fashionable shoes that cost $400? What you may initially have thought was just 16 hours of your wages now represents a whole week of your time. It's not a good exchange, and it's a lousy return on an entire week away from doing things that you might rather be doing, like crafting or being home with the kids.

And you might say to me, Jude, I want those shoes, and I'll wear them for the next year, and they will make me happy. And I would say back to you, okay. But they will be worthless, unfashionable and thrown away in a year or less. That money invested at 9.5%, the average stock market return (over time), will become $2,242 over 20 years without doing anything else with it.

In just one year, it would become $436. In five years, it would potentially become $615. And you then might say, 'Chickenfeed!' And I would say, sure, but apply it to everything you buy.

It's a choice that you need to make with every dollar you spend.

Every purchase you make today takes you further away from the time you could spend doing something you'd rather be doing. The things that will enrich your life emotionally and make you happy on a deeper level.

You should also consider how to get better value out of that hourly rate. Will it go up if you get a local job, work fewer hours and pay for less daycare? Less of a commute?

This isn't easy.

Start the mind games!

Aside from doing the exercises already outlined, start thinking about how and where you spend your money. *Every purchase commits you to more working hours.*

There is no end of money-saving websites available for you on the internet. A few good ones, aimed primarily at women, are listed in the resources section at the end of this book.

Limiting your spending is a mind game. You are playing just against yourself, so it's tough. You must be motivated to win.

First and foremost, you must decide that you do not care about what anyone else thinks. You are going to do your plan, your way, for your future. Full stop.

So, here are some ideas to win this mind game you are about to play.

- » Don't go 'shopping'. Don't spend time in shops unless you have to go there to buy specific things. Don't window shop, don't look at things for entertainment or go to shopping malls.
- » Do the same on your phone. Don't look at ads. Don't listen to testimonials and don't 'browse' magazines or flyers. Don't go to websites unless there is a specific thing you need. Buy and go.
- » If you need to leave your house for items, list what you need, buy those things and go home. If you didn't need it before you left the house, you don't need it now.

Why? Why do these things? Because everywhere there is advertising, marketing displays and enticements. There has been a great deal of psychological research going back decades into what makes people buy, and it is used ruthlessly by shops, marketers and display companies.

Do you think they don't know what presses your buttons that say 'buy'? They do. You will unlikely be able to resist their siren call until you are well-trained to ignore them.

For the shopping, you must do the following:

- » When shopping for food, set a menu for the week and shop for that. List what you need. This will limit the extras you buy while wondering what you *might* make during the week and will reduce the waste at the end of the week. Food waste is a monumental problem in Western countries.
- » When unpacking your groceries, write the cost of each item on the outside of the packet. When you throw it out at the end of the week, you will get a gist of how much money you are wasting on unused groceries.
- » Order your groceries online and avoid the impulse shopping that results when cruising the aisles.
- » Make slightly larger batches of things and freeze the extras. This will mean you have stuff on hand when you don't feel like cooking and you won't have to resort to a fast-food option. It will also allow you to

take something to work for your lunch, saving the spend on that.
- » Limit your purchase of alcohol. This is also hellishly expensive as a regular purchase.
- » If you are going out with friends, don't go to bars. Meet someplace where you don't have to drink or if you do, go to a BYO where you can take your pre-purchased alcohol. Bars charge you three to four times what the alcohol is worth before you go on to eat or go elsewhere. If you must go to a bar, limit your drink to just one or have a non-alcoholic alternative. All bars must have free water available, so that's an option, too. Money evaporates in bars!
- » Do not gamble or play the pokies. The house will beat you every time. Every time. A win will encourage you to put more money through the machine and the house will take it back. Ignore the pokies. Get your entertainment by watching someone else lose their money (preferably not your partner).
- » Limit your external entertainment. Once a week to a bistro or a cinema outing is okay; we aren't monks. But clubs, bars and concerts are high ticket items. You can put your money to better use. Put on some headphones and crank your favourite music. The effect is the same, and you don't have the crowd issue. (Spoken like a proper old person!) Really. Paying hundreds of dollars to watch an act in a stadium on monitors is a shocking waste of funds.
- » One of the greatest scams ever perpetrated on the population is the idea that wearing a brand name on your clothing is stylish! You are not a billboard. The fact that you are expected to pay extra for advertising a product that does not benefit you in any way is perverse. It might have been an interesting idea when it was a rare thing, but how cool can it be when every man and

his dog gets around in brand names like Champion, Nike or Tommy Hilfiger?
- » The other truly insulting idea of these designer brands is that they are made in the same low-wage, developing country as the stuff you turn your nose up at, probably in the same factory with only slightly better materials. It's a practice you are supporting. Please stop it. Seek out brands that are doing something about slave wages and lousy environmental returns if you insist on brands.
- » If you are still stuck on paying a premium so that other people recognise you as stylish, buy second-hand. There is a roaring trade in second-hand designer clothing that you can purchase. The people selling quality designer outfits are picky about the condition, so it will likely be in excellent condition with a much smaller price tag. You get the branding at a cut-rate price. That keeps it out of the landfill, at least. Seriously, do you think people can pick second-hand from new? Not on your life. Besides, when someone says, 'Hey, where did you get that cool thing by So and so?' You can look down at it and say, 'This old thing?' and know you still look fabulous at a reasonable cost.
- » A hint around online shopping, especially for apps and software: the seller often creates a sense of urgency by placing a time limit on your buying. Ignore this – it's a method to get you to buy.

With online shopping, especially app subscriptions, if you reject the first offer, it will be offered again at a massive discount. This is called a tripwire funnel. The thinking is: if you are reading, you are interested. If you reject the first offer, it is offered again at a massive discount. If you still reject the offer, you will be offered a lesser product for a tiny sum of money or even free. The object here is to get your email address, get you to buy *something*, and then continue to market to you relentlessly over the coming months. If you purchase something, hit unsubscribe on the first email they send you unless you are keen on the business because you WILL be hearing from them a lot.

And that, of course, is another issue. This relentless consuming. The cost of pulling it out of the ground, transporting it, sending it overseas to become something, then bringing it back at an inflated price only to be purchased, used slightly and then thrown away. We are choking on our own waste. It's not just about clothing – it's everything we consume. Plastics are in our oceans, chemicals are in our food, and pollution is in our water and air; it's desperate, and you have a role to play in addressing it.

Fast fashion is one of the biggest offenders of this – materials made from oil or natural products that need tonnes of poisons to be grown successfully. We poison our soil and water for the latest dress length or sleeve design.

Australians acquire an average of 27 kilograms of new clothing and discard an average of 23 kilograms of clothing into landfills per person every year.

It's estimated that the fast fashion industry produces about 20% of the world's wastewater and more CO_2 emissions than shipping and aviation combined. Clearly, hopelessly unsustainable.

Think carefully about this. Buy items that are made locally if you can. Made from organic materials – organic wool, cotton, bamboo or hemp, in styles that will last more than one season. Minimise.

Buy quality originals and support local crafters.

Some manufacturers and designers are trying to do the right thing. It's not a full-on movement yet, but a starting point that at least indicates an awareness of the problem. Sustainable clothing brands are emerging but aren't in the bargain bin category. This is a space to keep a close eye on. More designers and manufacturers are working on this problem – use your search engine to find those close to you.

There are many more, but now that you know they are out there, take your time and purchase thoughtfully.

All of this sounds like I'm hectoring you; I don't mean to. I am suggesting that we all have a role in getting better outcomes for our lives and the earth. They are not mutually exclusive. If you consume less and consciously consume, we will reduce the drain on the earth's resources while reducing the drain on our personal resources. Consume carefully. Think about what you are buying and why you are buying it. Is it an impulse? Walk away for 10 minutes. If you still think you want it, maybe it's worth your money. But if you have already moved on and are thinking of something else, you have escaped the clutches of the marketing people pressing your buttons. Do more of that.

Chapter 2

Living within your means

Where you live

Housing is at a critical breaking point in many areas with a severe lack of affordable, emergency and safe housing.

I can't solve those issues.

This is one of the highest costs you have as a buyer or a renter, and it's not easy either way. But this is an excellent place to start if you want to kick-start your savings program (which is critical to your future well-being). Not all options are suitable but examine your objections when considering them. Let's kick it around a bit.

» Don't rent the kind of house you'd like to buy. Rent something less than what you want. It will cost less and motivate you to save and move.

» Don't think your first home will be your forever home. It makes sense to move up as your current property appreciates, and you can afford a larger place. Get on the property ladder but do it where you can. Don't get yourself into an awful, stressful financial mess for your first home. Housing stress is becoming a real problem in the world.

Housing stress is when you are spending more than 30% of your income on housing. Currently, it is common for some purchasers to pay up to 60% of their income on a mortgage, and people still seem to manage. But that has been in an era of historically low interest rates. When the rates go up, this percentage of income used to meet the mortgage becomes untenable.

About a quarter of new loans have a debt-to-income ratio of more than six (this means six times your annual income), and of those, about two per cent have borrowed more than 10 times their income.

That means a few people with, say, $100,000 in income borrowed $1 million. At two per cent interest, which it would have been at the time, repayments were $4249 per month, or 60 per cent of take-home pay – painful but apparently acceptable to someone.

When the mortgage rate goes to five or six per cent (or higher, as it recently has), repayments will be at least $5369 per month, or 86 per cent of take-home pay. Assuming no immediate rise in pay, that leaves $220 a week for everything else. More than unacceptable. Untenable.

The long-term average in housing interest rates in Australia has been 4–5%. It has been as high as 18% and as low as 1%. But interest rates go up and down depending on the overall economy. Plan for around 4–5%, but expect some variation over the course of your loan.

Your lending institution is supposed to protect you by not giving you a larger loan than you can comfortably service. However, recently we had a heated property market, record low interest rates, and the whole thing went bang! with the pandemic. This has resulted in many property buyers with loans they are struggling to repay. Interest rates started rising at the same time as inflation returned and many families found themselves in a world of hurt. The other side of this rather nasty coin is that house prices may decrease as more distressed sellers enter the market. In that situation, you want to be cashed up and ready to buy.

If you think you can manage it, do your sums, considering potential rate rises.

> » Housesitting is not a practical solution for people with children but if you are on your own or a couple, this can save you a lot of money. It takes a while to establish your credentials but once you do, you can live rent-free for long periods moving from one gig to the next. It's not

a great long-term lifestyle but it's an option if you want to get your savings cranked. Registering as a house-sitter on designated sites costs a small fee but you can save thousands of dollars a year in rent. It's also a great circuit breaker if you are living with people (family or friends) to save but need occasional breaks from the living conditions. As a house sitter, it also allows you to try living in different areas or even countries with a lower cost of living. Treat it as an adventure. Put your stuff in storage (or sell it) and venture out.

» Try to consider all alternatives. Tiny homes, share homes, granny flats, caravans, the parents for periods to minimise costs and start your savings program. Everything is worth trying.

» Live with strangers. Okay, this is a little weird, but hear me out. Older people often own their homes in well-established areas. The homes are often too large for them (with empty bedrooms available). They still want to live there, but keeping up with the house is becoming an issue. There is a scheme near me where they match people who need low-cost accommodation (singles or single mums) and put them together with these older homeowners. The tenant (you) agrees to, say, 10 hours a week of labour: gardening, shopping or cleaning. There may also be a small fee for rent and ancillaries but it can be negotiated. This has great benefits for everyone. The tenant gets cheap rent in an established neighbourhood for little effort, and the older people can stay in their homes with the helpful company. Everyone wins if you can get along together – an option.

» If you can work remotely, another version of house-sitting is farm-sitting. People on farms need to holiday occasionally too, and you can use their place, often in great locations, for the price of you taking the time to feed the animals.

» If you can't afford a home to live in, get on the property ladder further down. Buy an investment property, something that can be rented out. It usually means a lower price tag, a loan of up to 90% of the purchase price and potentially some tax savings. If you are in a rising market, you will make money through the price of the property going up while someone else pays your mortgage. But do your sums carefully and make sure all costs are covered. Especially if the property sits vacant occasionally, you will have to make up the difference and pay the mortgage. I did this when I was ready to buy something just a few years after separating my financial affairs from my husband's. I couldn't afford a 3-bedroom house, so I bought an investment unit and rented it out. Over seven years, it went up in value. When I sold it, I had enough to make a deposit on two small units – one for myself and one for my eldest son. That, in turn, led to further investments down the track.

As a young couple in a cosmopolitan city, we always rented in nice neighbourhoods and had at least two bedrooms, even when there were just the two of us. We liked the room, and we always liked the neighbourhoods. Our first place was a one-bedroom unit in toffy Toorak in Melbourne. We soon moved on to renting toffy houses. But we paid the price for that. When we were ready to start our family and needed to save a deposit, we changed tack. We rented a one-bedroom house on a postage stamp of land in a neighbourhood just two suburbs away from where we had been living, but significantly more down market. It was tiny, and we were packed in like sardines, but no harm was done. I'm not advocating moving to unsafe areas, just something less flash than what you want. It's a great motivator. We saved a lot in rent, and 12 months later, we were ready to buy.

So, all that is about price, but let's talk about value. When we were renting as a young couple, I was in despair over the cost of housing, and that's when it was a fraction of the price it is now. I didn't think we would ever be able to afford anything, and if we did make a start, we would not be able to pay off the house in my lifetime. We lived inner city. We loved it. We were urban and taking everything the city had to offer. When we finally bought our first house, just weeks before our first child was born, it was an hour out of the city in a ramshackle mountain home with an overgrown yard and substantial gum trees down the back. Instead of needing the entertainment provided by the city, reshaping our home became our prime preoccupation – a labour of love.

We didn't have two crackers to rub together, but we set about improving our space, refinishing our bargain furniture buys, painting the walls and sanding down the floors.

Once we had secured the roof over our heads, we moved into the self-actualising phase of making it our own. It was a significant mind shift. Instead of theatre tickets, we were buying garden tools at garage sales.

We bought a house we could (barely) afford, and then we learned how to live well without spending money. Making the changes we wanted to the house with our own hands and ingenuity became part of our self-actualising journey. We lived there for six years. I loved that place, and so did the rest of the family we had created there, my husband and the two boys. It was different from the home we bought when we left it, but a business opportunity in Sydney could not be denied.

Chapter 3

Savings program and investing

The magic formula

Money should never be your sole source of motivation in life. But of course, to live where we live, we all need some income to pay for the things we want and need. So before moving up the pyramid, it's time to talk about money. How you make it and how you use it. This is the root of your future financial independence and subsequent self-actualisation, i.e. your happiness.

To successfully manage your personal finances, you need to understand two things.

One is that your expenses, which you must pay, must be less than your income. Happiness equals costs that are less than your income because then you at least can make some savings.

The second thing many people don't appreciate is the future value of money, which is the magic of compound interest.

If you save a little bit, quite small savings can make a big difference if you have time. If you have time, you don't have to make significant sacrifices. If you don't have time on your side, you will have to work harder to make the kind of savings you may want or need. If you save hard when young, you will be financially independent sooner.

I remember my university finance lecturer saying, 'If you take nothing else away from this course, tattoo this on your forearm 1 + i to the power of n.' That means your initial dollar (1) plus interest (i) over a number of periods (n).

I will do some simple math and show you how that works.

The idea of compound interest is that you get interest on your interest over time, so as your interest grows, your interest compounds. So, let's say you save $100 monthly over a year. And let's say the interest rate you earn on your money saved is 10%. (It's unlikely to be 10% at the moment, but it keeps the maths simple.) At the end of the year, you have $1259 because you have earned .83% on your money each month. As the interest compounds on the deposits, it can become like a snowball rolling downhill. It's incredible. In two years, you will have $2645 because your money is earning a little more each month you add to it. You have only put $2400 aside, but the interest is multiplying over time. In five years, it is $7744 (after savings of just $6000), and in 10 years, it is $20,484 (after savings of $12,000). I'll give you a better example.

It's common these days for people to buy at least one coffee from a barista during their day. These drinks start around $4 per coffee. Let's say you do that every day of the month, including the weekends. That adds up to $120 in the average month. But let's say that you save that $120 a month and put it in your piggy bank. At the end of the year, you have saved $1450. If you do that every month, ($120), for 20 years in your piggy bank you would have saved $29,000.

But that isn't what happens if you invest it. What do you think you'd end up with? The average return on the stock market has been 9.5% over time, so you can reasonably expect to get that if you invest prudently and leave it alone. That money invested grows to $85,431 in 20 years just for giving up one cup of coffee daily.

If you saved that coffee money and invested it every month for 40 years, you would have $652,344. This is theoretical because the stock market doesn't go up in a straight line. You have good years and bad years, but on average, the return over time is 9.5.

That, my friends, is not chicken scratch and is not a huge sacrifice. Now multiply that over the many incidental purchases you make, and it can make a massive difference to the end result.

If you understand nothing else I say after this time, all you need to understand is the magic of compound interest. It will make you rich. That's all you need to know. Small amounts saved over long periods can save you huge dollars.

This is the basis of superannuation funds or retirement funds. Put aside a little often and let the compound interest earned do the heavy lifting.

Remember it. It's super valuable.

$$1 + i(n)$$

Based on what we've just covered, you might be tempted to say, 'Right. I'll cut out coffee, and that'll be the end of it. I'll be fine.' Which is okay if you've got 40 years ahead of you of earning the same amount of money. If you don't, you will have to have a broader strategy. Also, maybe in the future, $600,000 isn't that big a deal. Based on today's calculations, you can't rely on that future value of money being enough. When I started my career, I won't say how many years ago, my annual salary was just four figures. I was making about $8000 a year, and that was enough. It's not anymore. It's not even close. So, you can't rely on today's value of money to be the same down the track. That's why you do more than just cut out the coffee.

Every dollar saved can earn you significant funds for your future.

Superannuation

Superannuation is the gift that keeps on giving if you let it.

Young people hate super because it is taken from their pay packet and won't be able to be accessed for decades. They feel retirement is forever away, and they need the money now.

Mid-career people hate super because they are focussed on gathering and paying off assets, raising kids and managing day-to-day life.

It's when you are entering your 50s that you start to think about retirement and whether you will have enough money to be comfortable.

Often, that is way too late.

People want to know how much money they need to retire comfortably. Well, when you're 40 years away from that date, it's an impossible question. But let's say you want access to 60% of what you usually live on. You would start as a young person putting 15% of what you earn into super. Currently, the Super Guarantee in Australia is only 11%, so you will have to do more to retire comfortably.

Superannuation is difficult because you want to save, but you want access to funds if an opportunity comes up to invest either in stocks or property. If you don't care about stocks or property, loading up your super can be a tax-effective strategy. You can contribute $25,000 per year to super. That includes what your employer contributes. Suppose your employer pays $10,000 per year into super for you. You can then salary sacrifice (this is an amount taken out of your pre-tax wages every payday) money into your super account. This has two effects. It lowers your tax paid on income (if you are in a high-income bracket, welcome relief) and increases your super funds, which are taxed at just 15%. This money will then collect compound interest for you in the years ahead.

If you can afford to save, invest, sock away or otherwise live on less than you earn, make it work either by investing in stocks, property or superannuation. Never let it sit idle doing nothing.

This is especially important for women because we sometimes take career breaks. Having children, supporting aged parents or taking care of a terminally ill friend, we need the backstop of additional funds to cater for these timeouts down the track.

The fastest-growing cohort of homeless people are women in their fifties. They are not as visible as the men because they sleep in their cars or couch surf. That is both shocking and outrageous but not that surprising.

Currently, 49% of Australian women have slightly more than $100,000 in their superannuation. There are still 22% of women in their fifties with no superannuation at all.[1]

When you are investing, and that is all superannuation is, you have

---

1   https://www.abs.gov.au/statistics/people/people-and-communities/gender-indicators-australia/nov-2019#economic-security

choices to make. Most super funds have a range of options depending on what stage of life you are in. For instance, if you are young, you may be able to invest in slightly higher-risk products than an older person because you have time to recover from any real downturns. If you are ready to retire, you will almost certainly take a conservative outlook. The table below shows ASIC's estimate of where these products fit. ASIC stands for Australian Securities and Investments Commission, a government body.

AGE	Growth Funds	Defensive Funds
Under 45	85%	15%
45-54	75%	25%
55-64	55%	45%
65 or older	40%	60%

Source: ASIC MoneySmart

This is the way ASIC indicates most investors should go. You must feel comfortable about your investment decisions based on your risk tolerance. If you are uncertain, contact your superannuation fund for advice. They are happy to provide it.

When you feel ready to do something with your cash, educate yourself as much as you can using reputable sources. I cannot recommend the Australian government's website MoneySmart (https://moneysmart.gov.au) highly enough. It is brilliant. It will answer all of your questions without pushing any commercial angle.

You need to consider how much money is enough to retire from work, either part-time or full-time.

This is where you need to work out how much you need annually to live comfortably. Today in Australia, if you own your home, a single person can live pretty comfortably on $30,000. It might be more or less for you, but that is average.

Of course, you cannot know how long you will live, so you should prudently plan to live on the interest or dividends from your investments and never spend the capital.

If you have $600,000 invested that is earning, say, 10% annually, then theoretically, you would be making $60,000 per year in interest.

Again, totally theoretical, and these numbers cannot be relied on as they rely on future conditions, not current conditions, and the stock market goes up and down.

A mix of interest income and pension allowances should give you a reasonable lifestyle. For instance, you have paid off your home and have a sum of money in superannuation. If you apply for the Aged Pension, you will likely qualify for a partial payment. This means that your super, converted to an annuity combined with the pension, will give you sufficient funds to live on, depending on the amount in your super. But you need a financial adviser to provide guidance based on actuarial tables and financial mechanisms. This is a constantly moving set of rules, so seek appropriate advice when ready.

The big takeaway is that you don't spend your capital if you don't have to. That is the money saved and invested. You spend the money that the capital makes. This is the terrible mistake that Lottery winners make.

It's the tale of the goose that lays golden eggs. You never kill the goose.

Chapter 4

Budgeting honestly

Everyone says budget, budget, budget, but getting started is challenging if you don't know how.

Simply, budgeting is understanding what you spend your money on. To know this well, you need to track your spending for a few months. A good exercise is to guess what you spend on things in a paper budget and then compare what you spend by analysing your bank statement. If you're good on a computer, download your bank transactions for a couple of months and categorise them.

If you're not so good on the computer, make a chart with columns and categorise your money. Add up what you spend in each category, like rent, food (groceries and eating out should be separate), entertainment, music, clothes, doctors, etc. Spend a couple of hours with your money habits to understand where you are spending and where you might be able to make savings. This is an exercise to know where you are spending now. This isn't a budget, although it will form the basis of one in the next step.

In most months, there will be one-off costs that aren't always in your budget. Birthday presents, insurance and one-off medical expenses should be kept to one side but tracked in a miscellaneous column.

Income is much easier to track. Add up what you bring in each month from one source or many. If you work casual hours, average what you bring in, but be honest. This is for your eyes only.

Creating a budget is easy. There are a lot of different tools online to help you do this – spreadsheets, tracking apps, etc. A great source of templates and information is MoneySmart,[2] a resource put together by the Australian Government. They allow you to download a budget template or to prepare and keep one online.

The first thing you need to do when sorting out your budget is to get everything on the same payment schedule. By this, I mean if you get paid weekly, pay your bills weekly; if you get paid monthly, sort your payments monthly. It makes it much more manageable. For example:

This is fictional Jen's first pass at her budget:

Item	Amount	Timing
Income	1277	Fortnightly
Rent	300	Weekly
Power	75	Quarterly
Food	60	Weekly
Gym	70	Monthly
Transport	40	Weekly

This is where she breaks everything down to the same period:

Item	Amount	Timing
Income	1277	Fortnightly
Rent	$300*2= 600	Fortnightly
Power	$75/6=12.50	Fortnightly
Food	$60*2=120	Fortnightly
Gym	$70/2=35	Fortnightly
Transport	$40*2=80	Fortnightly
Leftover	$429.5	Fortnightly

Get all your expenses into the same pay period as your wages or income. Then pay them that way. The power people don't care if you send them $20 a fortnight. It goes against your account, and there are no bill shocks once a quarter saying you owe them hundreds of dollars. Online apps make this simple. You don't have to pay your regular bills any attention at all, payday to payday as they are being paid automatically.

Where possible, add up the 'miscellaneous file' in your life and break

---

2   https://moneysmart.gov.au

those payments down the same way, by pay period. Then remove that money from your spending account into a separate account. This will at least give you a fighting chance to pay your bills each month and buy those little extras you need. This is stuff like car registration, annual insurance or holidays.

Now, a bit of discipline. Review your numbers. If you are confident they are realistic, decide how much you will save each pay period. You need to find some cuts if you don't feel you can save anything. Wind back on the outgoing payments and find some money to put aside.

If you need clarification about the approach to managing your money successfully, this is it and the order I feel it should be done.

- » Pay off all debt (excluding home loan if you have one) first. This costs you money and presents serious leakage in your budget. More on that later.
- » Save a nest egg for emergencies (at least $1000-$5000). Decide what is appropriate for you. Some people are comfortable with one month's expenses, while others advocate for an entire year. I feel that saving enough for 12 months of payments, while desirable, would feel at the start like a mountain too big to climb. But three months' worth of expenses available to you at call would give you absolute comfort in the case of an emergency or job loss. Start with saving your first $100 and go from there. It is very empowering when you have money in the bank.
- » Once that's done, save/invest like a demon.

Remember, every dollar you spend or propose to spend is committing you to work rather than doing something you might rather be doing. So be aware of that choice all the time. It will focus your efforts.

Create your budget. Be realistic. Allow yourself some small treats if it will help keep you on the path to savings, but don't let yourself off the hook too quickly. We're talking about your future financial health here.

Find a reasonable level of savings. At least 10% of your income is a good starting point. If you make 100 dollars, save $10; if you make

1000 dollars, save $100 – at LEAST. If you can't find this, review your spending budget again and find someplace to make savings regularly. Try to work your way to 30% savings.

Once you have identified your weekly saving, put it into a different account automatically. This is the key that so many people miss. In the bestseller The Richest Man in Babylon and numerous books since (like Profit First), they tell you to pay yourself first. What does that mean? Make some level of savings every payday. Skip the lunches out or cutback somewhere else to pay yourself first.

Your life and goals are why you work. Your family and friends are what bring you joy. Your financial independence is the most important goal. So, pay you first. If you don't think you can manage 10%, save something and work up to it.

That doesn't mean you don't have to meet your commitments. You do. You made them. As a responsible adult, you need to take care of the promises you have made to others – and that means financially too. If you try to renege on financial promises, you are making a big mistake. These things can follow you for a long time and make your life miserable.

So, you have started your saving.

You will remove one of your most significant budget leaks by paying off debt first. It will also give you enormous peace of mind once done.

To start, list all your debts from the largest to the smallest. Minimise your payments as much as possible to all obligations except the smallest one and knock it off. Then do the next debt. Commit as many resources as possible to the debt you are eliminating and knock it off.

This process gains its own momentum, but it's vitally important that you are not building new debt while you do this.

If you have credit cards, put them in a small container of water and put them in the freezer. This means they are available if you have a genuine emergency but are not available or carried with you for impulse purchases. Delete your credit card from your phone and stop waving your payWave card around! You will lose track of the money spent. Set a budget for spending and then carry cash. You will really notice it disappearing from your wallet.

If you have very high credit card debt or more than one large credit card debt, contact a financial counsellor urgently. Credit cards have very high-interest rates on debt, and you can be buried financially by them. Do NOT ignore high credit card debt. Get help. A financial counsellor can help you with a payment plan, assist in consolidating the debt and sometimes, negotiate to have the interest put on hold.

If credit collectors, loan companies and sheriff departments are already chasing you, see a financial counsellor URGENTLY. They really can help.

Being under this level of financial stress will damage your health, sometimes permanently. Take care of the issue and find your way back to normal.

The National Debt Helpline in Australia is 1800-007-007. It's free.

Continue to eliminate your debts, one by one, from the smallest to the largest. This shouldn't include your home loan at this stage, which will take many years. However, if you can find any extra to put against your mortgage, it will take many months and potentially years off the loan repayment. (See Chapter 8 for more on this.)

Once these debts are cleared, whether that takes a month or several years, you are set up for a better financial future.

Micro-investing

Through your budget preparation, you will know what it takes to run your life for a month financially. Plan to save enough to manage your life for several months and put it aside as your emergency fund.

You can put this money in an interest-bearing savings account or use one of the micro-finance apps on the market. Online banks generally give you higher interest with lower fees, so they are worth exploring. You can do an automatic withdrawal to your savings account directly every payday, and it will be available to you when you need it, within 24 hours, if not directly. This takes it out of your bank account, so you don't spend it.

I use micro-finance apps because they do good work. The one I use is called RAIZ in Australia. I'm not advocating for them in particular. There are others, but this is the one I'm familiar with.

I prefer saving this way for several reasons.

You have two ways to contribute: a minimum of $5 per week (up to any amount) and a rounding-saving program. The rounding savings come from the loose change on your purchases. This is a sneaky way to save money that you don't even miss.

The change is collected to one side when you use your debit or credit card (payWave) to buy something. When it adds up to $5, it goes into your account and is invested in shares.

For instance, if I buy something worth $5.27, 73 cents will get put aside (by the app). I then buy something worth $53.15, and 85 cents gets set aside. This goes on until $5 is saved and transfers into my RAIZ account. Loose change, but you never miss it; it adds up very quickly. This is a brilliant saving strategy.

» Your money is away from you and invested in shares.
» Your money earns dividends as the market rises or falls. For instance, over several months, I invested $1000 in my RAIZ account through regular deposits and my 'round ups'. In that time, I earned $440 in market returns and $105 in dividends. This is MUCH better than a simple savings account will get you. And yes, if the market falls, my $440 drops too. When the market recovers, it comes back. It DID drop in 2022 while there was much confusion around COVID, worker shortages, materials shortages and rampant inflation, but it's coming back now.
» The money is available at call but may take a few days to arrive in your account as the shares need to be sold.
» In an emergency, you can withdraw what you need. If you don't need to withdraw funds, it continues to grow.

With an app like this, you can decide what you invest in. This can include your beliefs through ethical funds only or whether you want to take a cautious or more aggressive investment strategy.

Set up your account so that as much as you can manage gets invested regularly. You will be astonished at how quickly this fund will grow.

Some friends I know use this as their Christmas fund. They start fresh in January, and by December, they have hundreds of dollars for their Christmas shopping.

Why is an app like this something I prefer to use? Well, it's investing small amounts into the stock market. Experts manage it, so you don't have to know much about investing to get the benefits and you will get a better return than just putting it in the bank.

Is it risky? Well, put it this way. The stock market will always be riskier than a bank simply because you are investing in companies, which are entities that can be affected by many external factors. But you still can choose a low-risk investment, such as bonds and cash. The safer your money, the less return you will get on it, so it's a decision you must make that no one can make for you. However, if anyone comes to you and says they can deliver higher returns than any other facility (banks or stock market) run, don't walk the other way. This is where unsophisticated investors get fleeced.

Do your research and decide what works for you.

The reason people lose money in dodgy investments is that they get greedy. Someone tells them they can earn higher returns than anyone else is getting. Or they are told of an investment opportunity they don't understand. If you don't understand the opportunity, don't risk your funds. Put them in a bank account with interest earnings and leave it at that. You need this money to be safe.

Each month, keep an eye on what you are doing. Visit your budget against what you are spending. Take every opportunity to manage your spending down and your savings up.

It seems a little obsessive, but an excellent way to encourage yourself is to look at this monthly and draw a picture on a graph. Your BLUE line will be your income. Your RED line will be your spending. The game's object is to get the blue line to go UP and the RED line to go DOWN so that you save more and more as time goes on. If you get a raise, keep it. If you get a windfall, invest it. If you win a small pool at cards (should you be gambling?), save it.

Seeing a picture of your success in graph form on the wall can be very motivating.

Take the time a couple of times a year to review the rates you are paying on loans, credit cards, power bills, mobile phones and internet, health care, insurance, etc. A bit of churn by changing companies gets you a better rate. If you don't want to change companies, find a better deal, ring up your supplier and demand the same value. They will often come to the party and meet the price of the competing supplier.

It can be helpful to join an online group, such as One Big Switch,[3] which works on using the power of a group to get better deals for members. It's free to join.

I remind you. This is a mind game. You will need all the resources available to you to stay on track. Temptation is everywhere. Someone is trying to sell you things around every corner and on every platform. Put your blinkers on and don't listen or watch. You have your goals. Save, save, save.

---

3   https://onebigswitch.com.au

Chapter 5

Using what you have

There are many ways to minimise your grocery bill if you are open to the idea. Think about what you are buying and become a shopping 'ninja' searching for the best buys.

For fruit and vegetables, try to buy seasonal produce grown nearby. We have become so used to purchasing what we want whenever we want it that we hardly think about the berries from Chile, the oranges from Florida or the frozen fruits from China. Not only will you pay more for these items but think of the transportation costs in terms of emissions.

If you can, purchase the 'less perfect' fruits and vegetables if they are offered in your store. Tonnes of food goes to waste because supermarket buyers think we will reject anything less than perfect. They are starting to stock the less perfect items for lower prices, so search for a supermarket that offers them near you.

Support your local farmers and work with what is available and plentiful.

The same goes for meats and small goods. Try to stick with local. If there is no local, go with regional, then country. The region first to minimise the carbon footprint. It might be worth buying a small freezer, going to a local butcher or farmer, and buying in bulk. This is an excellent option for getting a better price on your protein.

With canned and processed goods, we are fast losing our manufacturing companies due to large companies dumping their products on smaller markets. It makes it hard for our own companies to compete. But again, where possible, for all the reasons mentioned above, buy local or regional, even if it is a few cents more. You will reap the savings in other areas of your budget and save local industries simultaneously. Read labels and buy products grown and processed locally.

There is also the problem of brand snobbery. We become wed to particular brands because we have always used them, or we like their advertising or that's what Mum bought, but there are many no-name products on the shelf that are as good for less money. Where do you think these products come from? When a supermarket chain decides they want to bake and brand biscuits, do you imagine they build a factory? No! They go to the existing factory (if there is one) and ask them to make a slightly modified version of their bestselling biscuit as the no-name brand or house brand. The supermarket gets a good product, and the factory earns more, compensating them for any potential loss in sales of their branded biscuits. Not all no-name products are as good as their branded counterparts, but many of them are. And in many cases, the no-name brand has an acceptable quality for the application. Using canned tomatoes? Passata sauce? Jam? Pasta? Cheese? There is little variation in the products between branded and unbranded, so consider that when purchasing your grocery list. In some cases, the no-name brand may come from overseas. Be on the lookout for that and try to buy locally.

There is something else that needs discussing here too. Food use by dates. Here's an excerpt from imperfect-foods.medium.com:

> 'Best if used by' and 'best before' indicate when a product will be of the best flavour or quality. It's not a purchase or food safety date.
>
> A 'sell by' date tells the store how long to display the product. It's not a food safety date.
>
> A 'use by' date is the last date recommended for product use while at peak quality. It's not a food safety date, except when used on infant formula.

This has been a very controversial change in food labelling laws. By suggesting use-by dates, most people feel it cannot be eaten after that date. That is wrong.

Most things are safe to eat after their 'best by' date. They might not be as tasty or fresh, but they will not poison you. It just means they are past their peak freshness. Even that date is the best guess by the manufacturer.

When people throw out food labelled past its use-by date, they are often worried it will make them sick. It won't. When you get food poisoning, a pathogen is already in the food, like salmonella, E. coli or listeria.[4] If it smells bad, throw it out.

Otherwise, it's perfectly good to use.

Let's move to the cleaning aisle because you can make significant savings on your shopping list. In terms of cleaning, there is very little that cannot be achieved by having just five very inexpensive items in your home: white vinegar, baking soda, borax, Castile soap (in chemists) and lemons. I have a book at home called Home Made from Reader's Digest and it's fantastic for these cleaning recipes, but they are easily found on the internet.

There are some terrific resources. For local information, I use Electrodry. They are a carpet cleaning business, but if you check out their BLOG,[5] it's really useful for home cleaning remedies. There are many more sites on the internet. You can continue this with homemade recipes for shampoos, laundry soap, floor cleaners, facial masks, beauty creams and so on. No chemicals, all things natural and very inexpensive if you take the time to put it together yourself. Earth 911[6] is a site I particularly like, not just for homemade soaps and shampoos, but they can be presented as lovely gifts. Just letting you know that cucumber and yoghurt make a brilliant facial mask.

In terms of cleaning cloths, if you have old cotton sheets or t-shirts, cut them up. They will make better cloths than anything you can buy,

---

4   https://www.consumerreports.org/food-safety/how-to-tell-whether-expired-food-is-safe-to-eat-a1083080425/

5   https://electrodry.com.au/blogs

6   https://earth911.com

and they can be washed and reused or thrown if too messed up. If they get too mucked up for cleaning the house, pass them on for garage or workshop use. At least you were able to extend their life before discarding them.

Reuse your cleaning containers after washing them well. Try not to buy new ones! Make sure you label them well with your new cleaning products and what they are used for.

There are some products that cannot be swapped out. I use a particular brand of soap capsule in my dishwasher that extends the life of the dishwasher. I wait until I can buy this product in bulk at a discount before I top up my container. Significant savings can be made this way.

There are also many places where you can buy items in bulk using your containers. *This is only useful if you use the stuff.* There is no point in buying all kinds of stuff that will go to waste or be stored well past its use-by date. Laundry soap is a good one. Let's visit the laundry...

Many dry laundry soaps contain microplastics and filler. If you put a spoonful of powdered laundry soap into a cup of water, a percentage of it will never dissolve. This is the stuff that is going out into our waterways and making an environmental mess of things. So, I have an automatic bias against dry soap powders. A liquid laundry soap seems a noticeable improvement, but few list their ingredients for your examination. Read the label. Use a soap that is safe for grey water and septic tanks. That will make it a better option for the environment. Purchase soap with no phosphates. Instead of using a softener in your rinse cycle, use half a cup of white vinegar. It will cut any soap residue and leave your clothes smelling and feeling fresh (no vinegar smell, I promise).

While we're on laundry, how often do you wash your clothes? On my washing machine, the normal cycle is about an hour. So, for an hour, my clothes are washed, rinsed, buffed, squeezed and rinsed again. A lot of water and electricity for clothes that, frankly, are not that dirty. I wear them once or twice and wash them to freshen them up. I have recently stopped using the regular cycle on my clothes. I now use a 'refresh' cycle which is just 15 minutes. My clothes come out clean and smelling fresh, and I'm saving a packet on water and electricity. This won't suit everyone. Laundry needs a good clean and a couple of cycles to get the job done if you are doing messy or manual work. But if they just need a refresh, try a smaller cycle. It works.

Cleaning the bathroom is a job that no one enjoys but must be done. We drag out the bleach and plug our nose. It is not required. Soap scum can be dealt with by scraping the dry surfaces with a paint scraper and then wiped down with a slightly abrasive sponge. If you don't want soap scum, don't use bar soap. Use a liquid body wash instead. Bar soap uses paraffin to hold the bars together, and that is the residue in your bathroom.

The juice from a lemon can be squeezed into the toilet bowl, left for an hour and then scrubbed and flushed. If you have mould in your bathroom, firstly, improve the ventilation in the room. Mould is very unhealthy for humans. Secondly, spray the mould with a mixture of vinegar and water (50/50), leave it for an hour, and then wipe it clean. Apply a second time if required. Bleach doesn't kill the mould; it just turns it white so you can't see it. Vinegar kills it stone dead. We have been convinced we need these harsh chemicals, but we don't. Bleach has its place. But not around the mould.

Chapter 6

Big buying

How to buy things: traps for young players

Your first big purchase is usually a car. It is likely to cost thousands of dollars and represents your leap into the big time of spending. This is where people make their first big financial mistakes. Mistakes that can follow them around for years.

So firstly, you need to establish a budget for your vehicle. Not just what it will cost to buy it. You will need to maintain, insure, register and run.

Purchase	$ 5000	
Service	$ 400	At least. Plan to service your car twice a year.
Insurance	$ 500	
Register	$ 250	
Tyres	$ 160	You will need new tyres every 2-4 years, depending on how much you drive and how hard you drive.
Petrol	$ 80	A week at least.

Add it all together: $ 6,710. If you have $5000 cash to spend, you will need an additional $750 to get it registered and on the road. Then you will need an extra $80 petrol, $15 (service), $15 (insurance and rego) and $3 (tyres) per week to keep it running well at a minimum, assuming nothing breaks on it.

Don't take my word for it. My numbers are almost certainly low, especially for a young driver. Automobile clubs in your part of the world will be able to give you a far more accurate picture of the weekly costs of running a car.

Running a motorbike or scooter is less expensive but there is a significant upfront cost for quality leathers, boots and helmets, which are essential for safe riding.

If you need to borrow money to buy, you must convince the bank to lend you the money. This is the best value money you can borrow unless you can talk a parent into helping. The interest rate charged will usually be less than car lot finance or lease agreements. Make sure you understand the terms of the finance you are getting. How much interest will you be paying over the period, when the payments need to be made, whether early payments can be made, etc?

The bank will want to know several things:

- » You have considered your purchase and commitment to the bank to repay your funds.
- » You are a responsible individual and are aware of the running costs for a vehicle.
- » You will add at least 20% of the funds you need for the purchase. They will usually loan you less than 100% of the cost of anything.
- » You have a job or a savings record showing you have the means to repay the loan.

Once all that is sorted, it's time to think about what you want to buy.

Will you buy privately or from a lot? There are pros and cons to each. But when purchasing second or third-hand, it is all about '*caveat emptor*' – buyer beware.

When you buy from a car lot, the price may be slightly higher than you could get from a private seller due to the overheads, but there are usually consumer protections in place that are not available with a private sale. Check the company reviews online for customer feedback – ring local consumer advocate organisations. You can often bargain with car salespeople down from their starting price, too. If you go to the lot towards the end of the month, the salespeople are more likely to do a deal because they get paid commissions monthly based on their sales. Even so, it is worth doing your homework on what that model and year are doing in the paper, online and in private sales. It will give you a range for your negotiations. Be aware, too, that salespeople will seek to upsell you with 'coatings', add-ons and extras. Decide what you want, don't take their word for what you need.

If you buy from an individual, a little more caution is required. Many unscrupulous people will try to trick you into purchasing a vehicle that may not be what it says it is. For example, if you buy a stolen vehicle or a vehicle that has stolen parts, you may have that car confiscated by the authorities if you are in an accident or it is tracked down by law enforcement. So, when you are interested in a private vehicle for sale, it's essential to take your time, test drive the car and do a registration check on the licence plate and the VIN on the car engine. Local motor vehicle registration authorities are used to these checks, which can be made very quickly.

The VIN number is unique to each vehicle and can be found on the motor.

Don't fall for it if someone tries to pressure you to buy the vehicle before those checks are done. Better to lose the car than put your hard-earned money on something that can be confiscated with no recourse.

In some places, there is a cost to transfer the ownership of a vehicle. In Australia, stamp duty represents a percentage of the purchase price paid. Some buyers seek to lower the stamp duty paid to the government by asking the seller to falsify the actual sale price on the registration papers. If the seller agrees, you are both conspiring to defraud the government. Many people don't take that seriously. But if caught, you will face hefty fines.

I might seem like a real pill saying this because it can be a common practice in private sales. But you should never do anything to invite the state into your life. You don't want them there. Trust me on this. Live quietly and honestly and do the right thing. You have no power against the state. Once in your life, they can be reluctant to leave.

So, when buying a car:
» Spend as little as possible to get something functional

and reliable. Buy more with your head and less with your heart. If you buy a car you are 'emotional' about, you are potentially making a huge mistake. Why? Because you will buy something for more money than it is worth, and you won't see the faults in it or your logic. Take someone sensible with you.

» Buy something common. If you buy a popular model, you won't have any trouble finding a mechanic who knows how to fix it, and there will be plenty of second-hand spare parts around.

» If you live in an area that gets snow or is near the ocean, check carefully for rust around and under the car.

How do I know all this? Because I made all these mistakes. The first car I ever bought (in 1976) was a 1963 Mercedes 230SL convertible. Swish! At just 19, I took out a bank loan for a sports car I had no business owning. Unfortunately, I wasn't the emotional one – the adviser I took with me was! I wasn't even looking for a car, but he thought it was the deal of the century and convinced me to buy it. He was in love with it the minute he saw it. It was a private buy, and there was all the proper paperwork stating the thing was roadworthy, but it wasn't. The guy that sold me that car had a mechanic friend dodgy up the roadworthy paperwork. The car was breezy, but that was because of all the wind coming through the holes in the floor (that carpet and mats covered up). Once I got a really good look, I realised how close I came to being killed. The car was so rusted out underneath that if I had hit a decent pothole at speed, it would have broken into two pieces and disintegrated underneath me.

What to do? I had a car loan that would run for three years and a car that would kill me. My friend suggested I try to sell it on to the next mug. Well, I did place an ad to sell it, and a wonderful thing happened. I met a lovely guy who told me it was a pile of junk. I had to agree. But he said he had just fixed one up and sold it, and he suggested that if I trusted him to do the work, we would fix this one up together and split the proceeds. So over the next few months, Peter welded new steel into the frame and put in a new floor; I paid for a new convertible top, new fenders and a paint job. In the end, it looked terrific and was truly roadworthy, and we sold it. I was lucky to get out without losing my shirt. I probably broke even or lost a little, but lesson learned. Everyone is shocked that I owned a Mercedes convertible at my tender age. Ha! I've been much more sceptical about my car buying since. What was the second car I bought? An orange Datsun 120Y off a disposal lot for $1500. Great car.

Things to remember about buying a car.
- » Make sure the title is free and clear.
- » Buy the best car you can for the money you can afford. A used vehicle will always be better value than a new vehicle if you purchase with care.
- » It will never be worth as much as you paid for it again. A vehicle is an asset in name only. It loses money every minute you own it. Of course, there are exceptions to this, but very few! New cars lose money faster than used ones.
- » Make sure you can afford to run it. There are always unexpected repairs associated with buying a vehicle.

Even routine servicing of a new car will have to be done regularly, costing hundreds of dollars to maintain the warranty. There is nothing more useless than a car that is not running.
- » The better the car, the more your insurance will cost. If you buy a beautiful car, an absolute cracker, be prepared to have your heart broken. When I retired, I did buy a new car because it was my 'until I stop driving' car. Every mark on it has been made by another driver who didn't leave their details. Front fender hit, rear-ended, door chips and dents. Just saying…
- » Your car should be considered something other than a thing that gives you status. It is transport. Be canny about it.
- » Be careful. Not all sharks are in the water.

How to buy furniture

It's popular these days to furnish your whole place, bedrooms, dining and lounge from a single supplier. A 'total look' for your place that is cohesive and fashionable. Not only that, but you can also take it all home with you today and pay it off over three years. Interest-free!

Great, you say; sign me up!

A couple of things.

- » When businesses 'bundle' products, you often don't know how much you pay for each item. It allows them to charge more for some items than you usually pay. Not saying that's the case with all things, but when a business bundles, it is generally better for them, not you.
- » Interest-free does not mean cost-free. Ensure you understand all the fees included in purchasing this package. Costs could include establishment fees, payment processing fees, account-keeping expenses, annual card fees, etc.
- » When you buy a large package like this, they have sold

you on spending far more than you planned when you walked into the joint. If you had bought items individually, it's likely you would not have purchased as much as comes in the bundle.

» If the next three years go well for you and you can make all your payments, terrific. But who knows the future? Things like, I don't know, pandemics can come at you from nowhere. If that happens and you are late paying on your furniture package, that interest-free offer will turn into a monster. The lender is not obliged to remind you that your interest-free period is ending, and the interest rate on an unpaid balance can be as high as 26%.

» Do I need to remind you? You are enslaving yourself with your future time to do things that are not your favourite things to do. Life essence burned in advance for a lounge and dining suite or whatever else you have suddenly decided is essential to your lifestyle.

Options instead? Watch Freecycle, Facebook Marketplace and second-hand shops for quality items. They're out there. Second-hand furniture is quite hard to move when selling, so it's had all the overhead knocked out of it and will be at a fair price. Often older items are better made than the current furniture, which can be poor-quality chip wood stapled together. If you think the couch needs recovering, go online and buy a cover for $30. Then add a couple of colourful cushions for a relaxed boho look.

If you have young children, this is a better solution anyway. If you are frantic about the kids 'making a mess,' no one will enjoy using the furniture.

Chill out. Buy pieces that make you happy and don't enslave your future.

This can be applied to any large purchase, from computers to appliances to furniture suites. Buy only what you need and pay for it as soon as possible. This is good for the earth, too.

If you decide to rent furniture or appliances, send them back as soon as possible.

When my husband and I married, we hired a TV and a VCR (a new-fangled thing!) We couldn't afford to buy these items outright, so a small monthly fee seemed to make sense. Well, this rental arrangement went on for quite a long time. So long, when we finally said we would buy the items rather than return them, we had paid about three times over what they were worth! Keep an eye on rental items. Rental is only suitable for short-term use.

Buying a house

Buying a place to live is usually the most significant single purchase people make in their lifetime. It is more expensive than just the price of the house; thousands of additional dollars are often required to secure the property you want.

The fees I am outlining are standard for the most populous state, NSW. There may be slightly different rules in other states or territories. These are the major steps.

» Think about what you want within a budget you can manage. This generally means committing 25–30% of your income. If you go above that, and many people feel they are forced to these days, you may experience 'financial stress'. Financial stress means that you will be stressed paying your bills, you may lose sleep and your lifestyle will be extremely limited because all your resources will be going towards your mortgage. That's okay if it is voluntary (getting by with making extra payments when you can), but if it's daily anxiety, your health will suffer. This is the same issue if you are renting. Paying more than 30% of your income is debilitating. It's common these days but try not to. It is so damaging. It's lame to say. I know a lot of people are being forced to pay much more than 30% but do what you can to minimise that.

» Talk to a bank or mortgage broker about what you want and how much they will lend you. This is a complex process. They will want to know everything about your income, current debts, credit history and savings pattern. They want to lend you the money, but they also want to ensure it will come back with interest.

» If they agree, you will have a borrowing limit to go out and look for your property. They will insist you have skin in the game in the form of a deposit. How much depends on much of what you have indicated above, but it is likely to be a minimum of 15% of the purchase price. If you cannot save that amount or want to purchase with less deposit, you will have to take out mortgage insurance. Mortgage insurance is not cheap and is not there to protect you. It is there to protect the lender. You can expect to pay around $5000 for this sort of insurance. If you default on the loan, the lender is protected, not you.

» Explore what is available in government schemes if you are a first-home buyer. They are limited but know what's available to you.

» When you buy a home, you need to factor in additional charges. These include

» Legal or conveyancing fees to search the title. Upwards of $2000.

» Inspection fees – if you want someone to ensure the property is in good condition and to highlight repairs you will have to make, if any. Understand that even with a report, these people will not take responsibility for faults they may miss.

» Bank costs – depends on the financial institution. Sometimes these fees are waived but are often in the $500-$800 range.

» Stamp duty – the state wants a cut of the transaction. In Australia, stamp duty represents a significant cost of purchasing. It is calculated on a sliding scale and varies from state to state.

» NSW has just introduced the option of paying an annual land tax amount rather than stamp duty on the purchase.

Okay. Now you are ready to look for your property, knowing how much the bank will lend you. Seek advice from those who have bought a property as to what they think the priorities are. You may agree or not but do your research. Schools, transport, shopping, parking, one bathroom or two. All these things play a part; some will have to be traded off. Go online to see if there are infrastructure plans for the area you are looking at. This can be good or bad, but essential to know.

When I purchased a unit off the plan in Sydney, the information about the area was that there would be substantial investment in infrastructure in the coming five years, including a train station. That made it an excellent area for a rental property.

This is a decision you will be living with for a long time. Get a good idea of what you can buy in various neighbourhoods. Get a feel for the market.

» When you find a place you like for the money you can afford, contact the agent selling and make an offer. The first offer is usually below the actual asking price, sometimes as much as 10–15%. The agent will let you know whether you are in the ballpark. Use the agent for guidance, but don't take their word for it. The more the agent gets for the place, the better their commission is, so he/she is not acting for you. You can insist the agent puts the offer to the vendor (seller).

» This back and forth goes on until you either agree on a price, or you don't and move on. If you agree on a price, you must sign a contract with the agent and leave a 10% deposit. This takes the property off the market. There is now a cooling-off period where either party can change their mind. You may lose your deposit if the change of mind comes from you. The cooling off is generally five business days and the commitment can be cancelled. After that, you are locked in.

» Now you contact your lawyer or conveyancing company for them to get the information gathering underway. I use a lawyer because they read the contract and advise me of anything that is not standard or in my best interest. This is particularly important if you are buying a new property from a developer. You also contact your lender and let them know you will go ahead with a settlement in approximately six weeks. Generally, the lawyer, bank and agent work together to make this all come together in the background.

» Once you have made an offer on a property, arrange insurance. You don't want a fire to break out and destroy your place before you get into it. You don't know if the current homeowner has insurance, so there is no point in taking the risk. Also, arrange utility accounts to move across once you have a settlement date to ensure the house is functioning from the day you move in.

» Once a settlement date is set, you will be given your 'moving-in date', which is usually the same day, although not always. You will be told the time the settlement will happen. If it all goes as planned, you can pick up the keys and congratulations! You're home.

» If your interest rate increases or you struggle to pay your mortgage, you cannot simply walk away from your commitment. Your bank has no interest in you losing your home, so talk to them. They may extend the loan or adjust repayments to interest only until your position improves. If you are under mortgage stress, contact a financial adviser on the National Debt Helpline to get advice on the way forward.

Chapter 7

Women at work

Poverty traps

A recent report (2022) by the Workplace Gender Equality Agency found that the gender pay gap in Australia amounts to almost $1B a week. Why?
- » 33% is attributed to discrimination
- » A 6%–18% pay gap widens with your male co-workers as you progress in your career
- » An 11.3%–13.8% gap between men and women exists for those in the traditional and lower-paid female-dominated industries like healthcare, social work and education[7]

Add to those baked-in problems the issues of career breaks to have children, domestic violence, financial abuse and marriage breakups and women are behind the 8-ball before they start.

But that doesn't mean you get to say 'woe is me' and give up. It means you must work out what you want and how to achieve it, with a partner or without one.

If women have better financial outcomes, it's much better for the whole community. As women become stronger and more financially independent, they raise stronger, more resilient kids and put back into the community.

---

[7] Fair Work Commission awarded Aged Care Workers an interim 15% wage increase November 2022

Plan International[8] did a study a few years ago that proved it with an experiment in poorer countries. They would give a woman $100 in micro-financing to buy a sewing machine and she could start her own micro business. The follow-on from that was that $0.90 out of every dollar she made went back into that community in some way – in labour or spending or volunteering or the children or whatever, whereas it was somewhat less for men. So, no matter where you are, if women are resilient, financially independent and empowered, that flows to our children and our communities. It is incredibly damaging long term that there are so many working women raising children singlehandedly in poverty.

The object here is to show you what I have learned about saving, managing and growing your funds. This will give you choices when you need to make some harder decisions.

But there is also a broader thesis I want to promote. Our happiness is not just about money. Some of the poorest people in the world are happier than those in the West. That is often related to being part of a religious community, which relates to being part of community. Time and time again, studies on happiness indicate that wealth has nothing to do with it, although having your basic needs met sufficiently does.[9] Recent studies show that consumerism is actually damaging our happiness.[10]

Whatever you think, wherever you are, it's not too late. We should be aiming for a world where we are allowed to work less and focus on our hobbies or personal goals with enough money to see us through to our inevitable end. It's possible. But we have to start today.

It will help you. It will help the people you love. And it will help the planet.

If wearing labelled clothing is a giant hoax on the world's population, and I believe it is, then the myth surrounding the gig economy is a

---

8   https://plan-international.org/uploads/2022/01/biaag_state_of_the_worlds_girls_200_summary_eng_0.pdf

9   https://www.trackinghappiness.com/how-to-want-less/
    https://positivepsychology.com/happiness/

10 https://link.springer.com/article/10.1007/s12646-011-0065-2

shocking fraud. Dressed up as 'freedom', these jobs are the terrible result of the digital economy clipping your ticket every time you do a shift.

The so-called gig economy is where you work for a company that takes a fee for every job you do without taking any responsibility for your health or well-being while doing that job. It has been hidden under the cloak of 'convenience' and 'work for yourself' rhetoric while systematically stripping you of all the rights won by unions over the past 100 years.

What a crock!

This stripping of rights has now extended to many businesses and sectors where the catchphrase is now 'casual work', meaning that they do not have to pay you the hard-won rights achieved over many decades. Sick leave, a permanent job with regular hours, penalties for moving your shift all over the clock and the week, sufficient hours to live, a wage necessary to live, maternity and paternity rights, long service leave, superannuation, the list is long and outrageous.

People stopped joining unions, stopped understanding their rights in the workplace and didn't recognise the systematic stripping back of wages and rights until it was too late. The wolf in sheep's clothing had done its work. Supposed 'freedom' undid decades of hard-won benefits. Who better to take advantage of young people who don't know any better or women who are less inclined to negotiate? It spread like wildfire.

So, where we found ourselves was in a barren place. Workers, especially women working for wages that were insufficient to live on, with insufficient hours in a permanent location, with no job security, no benefits and no bargaining power. The gap between those doing the work and those benefiting from it financially has grown exponentially in the past decade. Shame on us.

And didn't the pandemic expose these workplace flaws dramatically? Casual workers unable to afford to take time off work, so working while ill; casual workers moving between two to three job sites to work enough hours a week to live, wage theft and middle-class families thrown on the welfare pile to their shame when they couldn't work. It was bedlam. This is what 'freedom' delivered to us.

And a wealth gap that is shameful between working people and some companies and business owners.

These gaps are beginning to be recognised more widely in Australia but the remedies will take many years to take hold, even if they are implemented.

So, girlfriend, you will have to act for yourself. There is a severe worker shortage out there. It's time to take the situation in hand.

- » Join a union. This can be expensive, and I don't say it lightly. Not all unions are excellent but they will give you a degree of clout that you won't have on your own. Someone will be in your corner with you if the going gets tough. Check out the movers and shakers in your industry and talk to your co-workers about their thoughts. This may not be your first move, but it should be in your kit bag.
- » Assess your skills and work experience. Get a professional CV or resume together. If you can't write it, get a friend to, or outsource it on Fiverr or Upwork. Find someone who knows what they're doing to write your resume and cover letter. Any errors in these documents will kill your credibility. Your CV can include skills other than those that come with education. Think about the skills you use daily and add them to the list. In the generic cover letter, say you are looking for new opportunities in your field and you want a permanent, full-time position. You can respond to ads or take the initiative and contact places you want to work.
- » If you have a pay scale in mind, keep it to yourself until you are in front of your potential employer. Have a figure in mind, but don't offer it. You may offer to work for less than they are prepared to pay. If they give you a figure that is less than you want, suggest the pay scale you are looking for. Be reasonable. If they offer more but still less than you want, but you want the job, say that will be fine, but you will expect

a review in three or six months. Three months is a standard probationary period for full-time work, so say you will expect a pay rise if you are both satisfied with your work. You are not a slave. You have power in this situation.

- » Project confidence but not arrogance. You know you can do this work.
- » Dress in what you think appropriate work clothes are. You don't need to wear a business suit to a cleaner's job, but you do for office work. If you don't have suitable clothing, some organisations will fit you. One is called Dress for Success, where they will find and give you appropriate work clothes for the position you are going for. They will also provide a level of coaching for your interview.
- » Professionally present yourself. Dress professionally and use appropriate language. If you have purple hair, facial piercings and tattoos, that's fine. All of these things are pretty common these days. But tone it down for the interview. This is going to inform their first impression of you. It's not about you and your freedom. It's about you representing their business to the public. Once they know you can do the job, they won't care as much about your personal choices. Be prepared to negotiate your look with them and find a middle ground everyone can live with.
- » Assess your workplace for advancement. Is this the sort of place you can build a career, or is it just a stepping stone? If you think advancement is an option, upskill in your time (or theirs, if they are open to it). Companies want to know that you are keen to be with them and are worth investing time and money into. Let them know you want to stay with the company and grow into higher roles.
- » Don't mess people around. If they offer you a position,

answer within 24 hours. If you are no longer interested, tell them as soon as possible. If you accept a job elsewhere, let them know.

» When you arrive for your first day of work, have all your documents ready, as there will be paperwork. Bank account for wages deposit, Tax File Number and Superannuation account. You can indicate which super fund you want to use, so don't let them tell you that you must use theirs.

» If you have moved jobs a bit, decide on your superannuation provider and consolidate all your super in one account. You can search for 'lost super' by entering that into a search engine. Your retirement funds will be far more valuable in one fund than in several. Make sure you are in a very low-cost super provider. Industry providers run by the unions generally have lower fees and better returns than commercial providers, but do your research and pick one that suits you.

Sometimes, the issue is finding a way to leave your employment without causing bad feelings. Your employer may have invested in you or be counting on you for a role. This was my situation when I decided to start my family.

I worked in the blokiest of blokey newsrooms in a high but not yet top-of-the-tree position. I was aware of being one of the first women to reach this peak in this newsroom, and I wasn't yet 30.

I fell pregnant with my first child a few years into the gig. I'm sure this confirmed all their fears in the blokey newsroom. Employ women and see? They get themselves up the duff! But so what, I thought. This is my life, and I wanted to have a baby, and I'd waited a while for this one to come along, so I was going for it.

I took maternity leave, and the baby arrived, and away we went. Within three months, I decided to return to work part-time. Partly because I loved the work, partly because I was worried that the newsroom would find a way to replace me. I found it stressful, but I managed. I was emotionally different. Footage that hadn't bothered me before with my compartmentalising brain could upset me enormously now. That wasn't easy. But I pressed on.

At the 1-year mark, I returned to work full-time. About a week later, I discovered I was pregnant with baby number two. Whoops. Hmmm, interesting conundrum. I was overjoyed personally, but I knew in my heart this was not a good look for my newsroom career.

I had a good long think about things. The work was stressful and emotional since I had my first baby. So, I devised my strategy. Early into my return gig, I went to the News Director and asked for a significant wage increase (we were about to negotiate my new contract). I cited baby costs, daycare, housing, etc., to the sizable rise I was looking for. He said he didn't think it could be done. Only because a new company had just bought the network and they were busy sorting out how to finance the purchase. I gave a deadline. The deadline wasn't met. I resigned.

It would have been awkward if they had met my demands because the plan was to leave. I just wanted to do it on my own terms and not reinforce the prejudices already present in the newsroom.

We parted amicably, and I went on to freelance and raised the boys with a less demanding job.

Do what you have to do for yourself, but also for the women who come behind you.

PART 2

PREPARE FOR THE WORST

Chapter 8

Let's talk about DEBT

Debt has become a way of life for many people. It is a way to achieve long-term goals, such as owning a house, or it can get you into a world of hurt if you have the purchasing power of a 35-year-old with low impulse control. Knowing the difference is the key.

It is always better to wait for your wants and save for it. Why? Anticipation. That dreaming of the purchase for long periods before it becomes yours. The gratification and satisfaction when it finally is yours. Expectation is hugely underrated. Try it out. Deny yourself occasionally.

There is good debt and bad debt. But let's first talk about the concept of debt itself. You decide to borrow from your future earnings to pay for your current needs. In many cases, this is useful. If you couldn't save up enough to buy a car when you needed a car for work, you could borrow against your future earnings because your car would help you make those earnings. This could be useful when you borrow the least amount required to get a car to fulfil your need and you know that your job is secure and that future payment will be met with earnings.

This is still an example of bad debt because what you buy is going down in value. So, you will pay over time for something worth less than you paid. Not clever, but sometimes necessary. This was the sort of debt you went to the bank for. They would give you a sum of money and allow you to pay it off over time (usually one to five years, depending on the amount) with an additional charge of interest, which was how the money lender (the bank) made its money. It is not the same equation for saving 1+I over (n) periods because that involves compound interest.

This is *simple interest*. The loan amount and the interest being charged are broken into equal payments over time.

This equation is Interest = P(principle), R (rate of interest) and T (time) or I=PRT.

Your repayments are initially a large part interest and a small part principle (the sum borrowed). The interest is high at the start because it is being calculated against a high sum of borrowings. The more payments you make, the more the balance shifts to paying off the principal and getting lower interest bills.

It takes a long time to build equity in your home because all the money for the bank is made early on.

This is what the loan/equity looks like on $100,000.

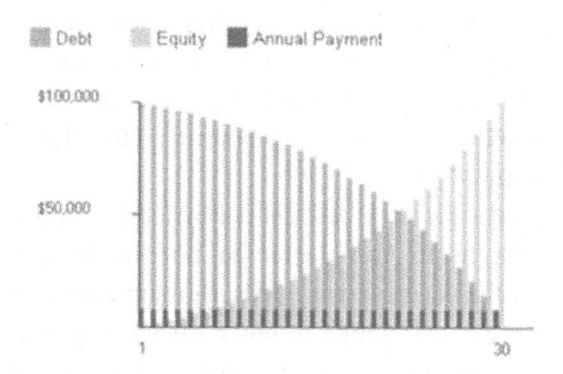

Even so, in all cases, it is better to pay off your loans as fast as you can.

So what happens if you pay additional amounts of money on your loan? It goes away a lot quicker.

Let's say you have a loan for $300,000.

The interest rate is 3.88% over 25 years.

You will pay $1643 per month on a set day of the month.

If you add another $80 per month to your payment two years in, you will save $12,352 over the life of your loan, and you will have it paid off one year and eight months earlier than before.

Now, let's look at things another way. You have a loan for $300,000.

The interest rate is 3.88% over 25 years.

This is the same loan as above, but you decide you will pay $761 fortnightly (rather than monthly) as you get paid every other week.

Again, if you add another $40 per payment two years in, you will save $13,299 over the life of your loan and repay it one year and 22 fortnights (about five months) earlier.

You will pay $380 per week, save $13,305 over the life of the loan and have it paid off one year and 10.5 months earlier.

Amount	Interest	Paid	When	Saved
$300,000	3.88	1723	Monthly	$12,352
$300,000	3.88	801	Fortnightly	$13,299
$300,000	3.88	380	Weekly	$13,305

Use an extra payments calculator[11] to see for yourself!

Borrowing from a bank or mutual society generally gets you a lower interest rate than any other form of borrowing. Bank loans are generally used for long-term borrowing – 3–30-year terms.

This is where credit cards bring people undone. Some people view credit cards as a convenient form of credit, and they are for very short-term loans.

Credit cards are the highest-cost money you can access in the legitimate money world. Credit cards should be used only for purchases that will be paid off the next time you receive your bill. Where a bank might charge you 8% or more for a consumer loan, a credit card will often charge you an interest rate into the high teens or 20s. 24% is not uncommon. Easy credit is a debt trap. If you cannot pay off your debt, it multiplies. The following month, it multiplies again (assuming you haven't added more to the card), and the next month, it multiplies again. This can be ruinous for people who are unprincipled spenders.

In severe cases, if the bank (or card owner) can't get their money from you, they sell the debt to someone who will. Those people will hound you, turn up at your home, your work and phone you constantly.

If your credit card is from a bank, you may have some protection

---

11 https://www.macquarie.com.au/home-loans/home-loan-calculators/extra-repayments-calculator.html

under consumer law. This will depend on where you live. But don't buy, hoping your bank will bail you out. They won't. Charging interest in products is one of the ways they make their money. Never stand between a banker and his money! Applying for credit cards and using them is just digging a financial hole for yourself while they hand you the shovel. (They will object to that description but it's my opinion.)

If you are in a situation like this, get financial counselling help immediately. Don't try to manage it yourself. It can be highly stressful.

This is what happened to me.

I had just started at my dream job. Things were going well, and I was enjoying the work. My husband was also working, and we were trying to get back on our financial feet after a business failure. Things were looking up.

My phone rang while driving and I answered on the hands-free kit. Yes? It was a debt collector. I had separated my financial affairs from my husband, but this card had an outstanding debt from our joint account for which I would be held responsible. The debt was $14,000 on a card I had never seen or used.

I pulled over to the side of the road to concentrate properly on the call. I had no idea where I would pull $14,000 from, and I knew my husband wouldn't be any help. His solution was to ignore these calls. That's why I was getting them.

I was shattered. The debt collector said they would ring me back in a couple of days while I thought about what I could do.

I was sick with worry and confronted my husband about the debt. He wasn't concerned, but his lack of concern was ruining my credit rating and I cared about that.

When the debt collector rang back, he was sympathetic. They must come across this all the time. I explained how I didn't know how to repay it except over time. The collector sighed. He said, could you do $5000 over a couple of months? With belt-tightening, I thought I could. 'Yes, I think so.' Well, he said, don't think so. Do it and the debt will be resolved.

I did.

What I learned here was a couple of things. Firstly, my husband was hopelessly financially irresponsible and I had to fend for myself more strongly. Second, when a debt is sold, in this case by a bank to a debt buyer, they sell it for pennies on the dollar. If this debt collector bought the debt for $.10 on the dollar, he paid $1400, betting he could collect at least that much against the debt. The bank writes it off as a bad debt; the debt buyer works on collecting the debt and, for a $1400 outlay, makes a profit of $3600 (on the deal we did) with a few phone calls. The debt collector can decide how much will cover his time and trouble.

I was lucky. I got a good guy and he let me off the hook. He made money, I cleared the debt and we all got on with our lives – a professional debt buyer worries about large sums, not our petty $14,000.

Other debt collectors are third-party agencies hired by creditors to collect from non-paying customers. These are known as 'Contingent Collectors'; many do not care about the rules. This is debt collecting outsourced to agencies that will harass you even though they often deal with people in vulnerable circumstances.

This is something a financial counsellor can help you with. They can consolidate your debts into a single payment, they may be able to negotiate down your debts, and they can teach you how to get out from underneath.

Only some of the time, however. There is no specific legislation covering the debt collection industry, just guidelines. (And you know what Jack Sparrow[12] has to say about guidelines…) They are not legally enforceable rules.

Debt collectors sometimes completely ignore the guidelines set by the ACCC (Australian Consumer and Competition Commission) and ASIC (the Australian Securities and Investments Commission).

You've been warned.

Credit cards used to be used rarely, only for big purchases, like appliances or emergencies, like car repairs. But debt has become so normalised in our daily lives that many people have so much credit card debt that they cannot see the light beyond it.

---

12 Jack Sparrow is a character in the Disney *Pirates of the Caribbean* movie franchise. One of his quotes was about the rules around 'parley', not rules so much. More just guidelines.

Enter a new form of debt that is even more insidious: the Buy Now, Pay Later (BNPL) products taking the market by storm.

Back in the day, if you didn't have money or a credit card, you could put things on layby with the cooperation of the retail store. You would pick out your product or products and the store would put them aside as you paid them off weekly within a set period. After they were paid off, you collected them and took them home. This was the alternative to using credit cards or getting a loan, and it's still available. Women used to do their Christmas shopping months early and put the items on layby. Appliances and furniture were also everyday items to put on layby. No interest is charged, but you must pay the things off within a set period. The motivator was that you didn't get your items until all the payments were made.

BNPL is based on that principle but is different and much more dangerous. With BNPL, you get your items now and pay them off over four periods. This is a new-ish product, on the market since 2015 and aimed squarely at millennials who want it now and will worry about the money tomorrow.

If that is you, they are setting a trap for you. There are some critical differences between BNPL services and credit cards.

- » When you apply for a credit card, there is generally at least a cursory check as to whether you can afford to repay a credit card debt. BNPL services do not do this check.
- » Credit cards can be paid off over time but incur high-interest rates if the debt is not cleared. BNPL services must be paid over just four payments (usually eight weeks) and will incur a penalty fee if a payment is missed. If two payments are missed, the price goes up. In some countries, there are caps on the penalty fees. I don't know if those penalty caps exist everywhere.
- » With both services, you are spending future income. In uncertain employment, you risk going into debt that can spiral out of control.
- » With credit cards, there is a limit on the card (except

American Express). With BNPL services, there is no limit. With these services, you could dig a good-sized financial hole in no time.

The average transaction for a BNPL transaction in Australia is about $150. They promote their service on the basis that there is no interest. However, there is often a fee for just having an account.

If you purchase $150 and miss a payment, you will incur late fees with an effective interest rate of 28.25%. One local BNPL will charge you an effective rate of 49%, a staggering sum and well above what most credit cards will charge you.[13]

We could debate all day about the value of BNPL against credit cards or bank loans for large purchases. However, I have found it deeply disturbing that young women get their hair done in complicated configurations using BNPL services. Nails, beauty treatments and ephemeral treats will be long gone before the debt is paid off. It's crazy and money foolish. Indeed, if you can't afford your hairdo, leave it alone! Special events, sure. But your everyday look? Yeah, nah.

You have spent your money before you have earned it. We are back to the concept of spending your future time and earnings on something that is transitory. This sort of spending will send you backwards.

There are moves to set firmer rules around the BNPL providers, so watch this space.

Payday advances

Don't. Just don't. This is desperate. If you are desperate, you can't afford to do this – financial suicide, in my view.

If you need help to get your finances back on track, talk to a financial counsellor. They offer a free and confidential service to help you sort out money issues.

National Debt Helpline – 1800 007 007

---

13 https://www.thenewdaily.com.au/finance/consumer/2022/07/21/buy-now-pay-later-credit-card

Chapter 9

Money and partners

This is a tricky part of the savings equation because partners sometimes have differing views or don't agree to the same extent on the goals you may set. In The Barefoot Investor, Scott Pape recommends a regular date night to discuss goals, money issues and how you want to get there as a couple. This is a great idea. Unfortunately, this was not a process we thought of, and I suspect my husband would have been reluctant.

My experience is already on the page. My husband and I had similar financial goals – we wanted to be well-off but disagreed on how to get there. He was acting well-off while waiting on the 'big breakthrough'. I was working away on incremental improvements. We went through the boom/bust sequence a few times, but in the end, the situation resulted in less boom and more bust.

If you are confident that you and your partner share the same goals and agree on the way forward, go for it. Blend your money, join forces and go with God. Unfortunately, I know of too many cases where one walks out on the other, taking the 'nest egg' with them.

I also know of many cases where one partner has relied on the other to manage the money only to discover that they had no plan and no provisions for their old age. This is not unusual. If you do not ask the question and demand an answer, you won't know. It is imperative that you understand your financial situation.

Money is a funny thing. When it is theoretical, people believe they will behave a certain way.

'If we broke up, I would always make sure she got half of everything.'
'When we sell the house, we will split the proceeds down the middle.'
'I don't care about the super.'

Understand this. When money is theoretical, it's easy to believe you will be and will treat others fairly and equitably. Once it is no longer theoretical, i.e. the money hits the bank account, all bets are off. People suddenly find all sorts of reasons that a split down the middle or whatever else they proposed previously is no longer what they intend. And very often, unless you are prepared to go to court (an outrageous expense on its own), there is not much you can do about it.

This is borne out daily in the courts and homes around the nation. So if you are going to create a 'nest egg' or have a partner in your financial affairs (personal or business), please put safeguards in place – dual signatures on accounts, both names on property deeds, no additional credit cards against accounts. And don't just take someone's word for it. Go with them to your bank/solicitor/JP to ensure these safeguards are in place.

Your partner may get cranky, suggesting you don't trust them, but trust is earned and it works both ways. You both need to be completely comfortable that the other will be involved in any financial transaction around your accounts. This is to protect them as well. If they object, be careful what you agree to.

Love me? Pay me!

There is a disturbing trend towards online romance scams ramping up at a rate of knots. Women are often the victims of these online scams, which amounted to over $547M in 2021 in Australia. False profiles encourage people to exchange personal details, financial information and emotional needs with strangers they have not met face-to-face. Even face-to-face is no guarantee. The scams in all age groups are going up yearly in this area, meaning the scammers are becoming increasingly sophisticated. The Moneysmart website highlights the four indicators that your 'romancer' may be a scammer:

So how can you spot scammers if you're looking for love online?

» Nobody legit will ask you to help by sending cryptocurrency, giving the numbers on a gift card or wiring money. Anyone who does is a scammer.
» Never send or forward money to someone you haven't met, and don't act on their investment advice.
» Talk to friends or family about a new love interest and pay attention if they're concerned.
» Try a reverse-image search of profile pictures. If the details don't match up, it's a scam.

It isn't terrific, but you must protect yourself against less honest people – question everything. Be careful. This will determine how you and your children, if you have them, will live in the future.

If your new 'lover' needs to be funded by you, is that what you're looking for? Move on!

A final note when working online? Put protections in place. Data leaks are announced daily from businesses that may have your personal and financial information. I suggest three simple things.

» Get a software password vault. These create long, complicated, unique passwords that no one will guess. With the app on your phone, you access it before going online, and your passwords are readily available. You don't have to try to remember them.
» Put 2-step verification in place for your online accounts. It's no big deal to wait for a 6-digit code from the site to confirm you are who you are.
» Lock your mobile with a password or fingerprint.

Online accounts and the internet have allowed tremendous changes in how we manage our daily lives. It's a lot more convenient. But that convenience comes at a cost. Protect yourself because no one else is going to.

Chapter 10

Financial disasters and abuse

I want to talk about building resilience. We are often forced to be strong beyond what we imagine we are capable of simply because there is no alternative.

We must work to build this resilience because whatever your situation, you will need it.

No life is lived free of adversity. If you are in the world and connected to people, there will be tragedy somewhere in your travels.

But you must not let it define you. It will side-track you. It will distract you. But it must not derail you. Never, ever view yourself as a victim.

My first encounter with financial disaster was when I was 11. I asked my dad, who was home from work with flu, what household items I could use to make my first aid kit. I was going for a Girl Guide badge. I collected the items, went into the next room and began putting them together. My dad started to cough. A little at first, then a lot, then nothing. My mum was yelling at him to breathe.

A frenzy of activity with siblings, relatives, neighbours and rescue personnel took over the house to no avail.

And just like that, our world was turned upside down and inside out. My mother was suddenly widowed at 32 with five kids to support. Our circumstances changed in a heartbeat.

My dad had run his own business, so the funds were frozen and we were suddenly people with no money. It was resolved eventually, but I clearly remember being told there was NO MONEY. And why would there be? Who expects to drop dead at 39?

Our ducks were far from being in a row. I suspect they were cast all over the half-acre we lived on. Building a business, buying a house and raising five kids. Whew. The panic my mum experienced must have been epic. No current work skills, overheads, a business to sell and kids ranging in age from 4 to 15. Perhaps there was life insurance, but I don't know. Something changed because within a couple of months, after relying on uncles and aunts coming around with casseroles and bike repair kits, we had adjusted to our new circumstances. We still had no money, but we stopped talking about it.

So, what can you do? Prepare for it. You will not be spared. You need to be ready to support or be supported through times when you are tossed through the rapids of life and thrown up on a rocky bank somewhere. If you have your financial ducks in a row, you will have choices available while you cope with disaster.

Disaster can take on many forms. Illness. Death. Job loss. A legal drama. Family issues. Divorce. Injury. Pandemics.

But there is more to being resilient than just having funds available. Yes, that's important, but you will also need emotional resilience. This also takes time to accumulate. So, from a distance, these are my recommendations.

» Learn to step back. From everything. Allow yourself to sit quietly (actually or metaphorically) and stop the noise. Opt out of the news, turn off your social media and spend a little time with yourself. You don't have to wait for a crisis to do this. It's essential that you get some practice in before you need the space. Learn how to find it quickly. Meditation? A run? A warm bath in a darkened bathroom? Journalling? An excellent piece of music? Explore and try things. People talk rather glibly about mindfulness, but you must find this place within yourself. Natural emotional mindfulness is being in that space, in that time, with nothing else intruding on your thoughts. A place for you to rest.

» Find out who you trust, really trust, with life-changing information. Someone who will listen closely. Someone who will not judge you. Someone you know will tell you the truth. Someone who will not pass on your information without your permission. These people are vital in a crisis. If you have one, great. If you have two, even better. If you don't have one, maybe work out why you don't and see if you can rectify that situation. Nurture the friendships that matter – and that means being all those things back to someone. No sharing secrets that have been gifted to you in trust. I say it's great to have two because you will need to talk through your tragedy over time. It's better to share the load with a couple of friends. I had three people I shared with when my marriage was in crisis, all in different time zones! Two of these women had never been married themselves (perhaps reflecting on a lucky escape!), but they listened, counselled, supported and we all got through it.

» Shake out the bad ones. The other side to finding people you can trust is to ditch the people you are in touch with but don't like. These people will sap your mental and emotional strength. If you are not being supported or encouraged by your friends, if they don't agree with your goals or aspirations and denigrate you for having them – walk. These people are everywhere and they will make you feel bad about yourself. Don't let them. Clean out your friendship cupboard. It's highly effective as a way to feel forward movement.

» Face your fear. Think of something you are frightened of. Take a baby step towards it. Examine yourself for damage. None? Then take another baby step towards your fear. The more you do this, the stronger you will feel. You need to learn to trust yourself. Your capability. Your judgement. Your strength. What could this look like? This is the basis of one of my favourite expressions. 'Feel the fear, but do it anyway.'

» Do something by yourself. If you are always waiting on

others to do the things you want, stop. Teach yourself to go alone. Movies, parties, travel, lessons. Don't put your life on hold for other people.
- » Start something. Have you wanted to try a side hustle? Volunteering? Singing lessons? Entertaining? Writing? You can't get better until you start. Start small. Learn. Try again. This is how everything starts.
- » Learn something. Back to school to learn what? A trade? (Pretty useful these days!) A degree? A long, put-off dissertation. Expand your brain. Refresh your outlook. Meet new people. Refocus on new horizons.
- » If you feel stuck, get unstuck. Only you can decide what you want and then go after it. These are all things you can do to build your strength and trust in yourself. You will need reserves when you are faced with difficulties.

I needed all these tools and more when our family suffered a sudden death. We lost baby Brooklyn Jean at just 15 weeks old from SIDS. This little girl was full of life and personality until the evening she just stopped breathing and couldn't be revived.

Grief will eat you alive. It is such a powerful, debilitating emotion. It saps your strength and makes you question your will to live. But there is still work to go to, children to feed and dress, and days to get through. So, you have to find a way. The other tough thing about grief is that the rest of the world moves on while you struggle to overcome an emotional gap that cannot be filled.

For me, a road trip sets my head straight. A few months after her death, I took myself away on a month-long camping road trip. I needed to drive to exhaustion, howl at the moon, sing at the top of my voice while the wind was in my hair and spend some crazy, quiet time on my own. In 28 days, I travelled 6500 km. When I came back, I cleaned out my friendship cupboard. I felt better.

There is something about loss that won't allow you to put up with other people's bullshit anymore. You never get over the loss; you must learn to accommodate it. But it makes room if you clear out the rubbish being stored there by other people. Put it down. Walk away and don't look back.

The very common story of financial abuse

I hear you saying, why didn't you leave your husband over this financial stuff? I'll tell you. I never thought marriage should be about money, although it is the cause of the failure of many partnerships. I put up with his financial shenanigans for too long, but I was finally on my way to extricating myself from his constant financial disasters. I thought that might renew our marriage commitment to each other.

Why do we stay with partners that take advantage of us? I know another very smart, professional woman friend who said, 'Jude, I can be right, or I can be married.' For a long time, she chose to be married. Then she decided it was time to be right.

Sometimes, we are just too frightened of the alternative. Living in fear is a lousy way to go through life.

I re-read my vows repeatedly during my marriage because I believed in them. I was an ant, and I'd married a grasshopper.[14] But I knew he was a grasshopper. He took me places and we did things that I would never have done by myself. I would probably not have bought the ramshackle house in the mountains, which I loved. I would not have helped start the tech business that had us flying too close to the sun, melting our wings. I would not have flown business class from Canada to Hong Kong over the North Pole drinking Napoleon Brandy. These things are part of my most treasured memories of our life together.

I wanted to believe that I could solve the money issues. A marriage is much more than money; I strove to solve the problems.

Twenty-one years into our marriage, he was arrested for embezzling funds three years after I had separated my financial affairs from his. Almost three years later, at trial, he was sent to prison. We were formally divorced within a few months of our 25th wedding anniversary.

Not because the marriage was about failed money management. But

---

14 Aesop's fable of the Ant and the Grasshopper is a story of selfishness. The ant saves for a rainy day while the grasshopper enjoys each and every day doing what he wants. During a particularly cold and harsh winter, the grasshopper asks the ant for assistance. The ant refuses because he resents that the grasshopper fooled around while he worked. Lessons for both sides here...

because I had been trying to fix something he didn't want to be fixed. In the end, the shared values and mutual respect were not shared or mutual.

A story about values

I saw this on Facebook. I don't know who wrote it, but I loved it and repeat it here:

> A father said to his daughter, 'You have now graduated with honours. Here is a Jeep I bought many years ago. It is pretty old now. But before I give it you you, take it to the used car lot downtown and tell them I want to sell it and see how much they offer you for it.'
>
> The daughter went to the used car lot, returned to her father and said, 'The pawn shop offered only $100 because it is an od Jeep.'
>
> The father asked his daughter to go to a Jeep club now and show them the Jeep. The daughter then took the Jeep to the club, returned and told her father, 'Some people in the club offered $100,000 for it because "it's an iconic Jeep and sought by many collectors".'
>
> Now the father said to his daughter, 'The right place values the right way.'
>
> If you are not valued, do not be angry, it means you are in the wrong place. Those who know your value are those who appreciate you. Never stay in a place where no one sees your value.

PART THREE

INVEST IN YOURSELF

Chapter 11

Stepping up the hierarchy to safety/belonging

The reason home ownership is so vital to a community is that it creates cohesion. If people are buying into an area, they care what happens there. They get involved. They participate. And they will take action when things they don't like happen. This is the basis of society. We follow the same rules so we can all thrive. It can work for renting too, but the stakes are not nearly so high.

One way or another, hopefully you have your housing sorted and are now part of a community. This is where we start moving up the pyramid of needs. You must go out of your way to integrate with this community. You don't have to elbow your way into people's lives, but you need to exchange greetings and help with small tasks. This is not someone else's job. It is yours. You are the newcomer. Make sure your neighbours know you are friendly and caring. Be pleasant.

Many people find this integrating part confronting, but it doesn't have to be. Go at whatever pace suits you, but don't ignore the people around you. This can be misinterpreted and will lead to suspicion and bad relations.

Chat with your local store owners, wave hello to your neighbours and find a place to volunteer if you have the time.

This is important because, after your basic needs of housing, security and safety are met, the next most critical need is community, a sense of belonging. You don't need to invite sticky beaks into your life, and you don't need to become one. Gently integrate. It will lift your daily spirits in a surprising way and eliminate that sense of loneliness and alienation that is so common in the modern world.

Don't take your community just from your workplace because you might leave that work one day. Then what? Build your community all around you, wherever you go.

The internet makes this much easier to do than it used to be. Look up volunteering opportunities in your area, search the local council site, look for sporting clubs, community groups, singing groups or choirs (singing is so good for your sense of well-being), classes, conservation groups, and anything that you have an interest in and find like-minded souls to do it with.

This is also a helpful way to explore the possible options for a side hustle you might want to start. Do you have a craft product you can sell in a local shop? Could you teach a class on something? Is there a need for your skills when you take a look around? Look up side hustle ideas on the internet (there are thousands of them) and determine what might help you in your savings program. Boost the blue line on your wall graph!

This is where your loving and belonging need comes in on the hierarchy. It is vital to our well-being. It is also where your self-esteem, status and recognition expand beyond your workplace. You are part of something bigger. Digital friendships are fine. In-person friendships are better.

From a very young age, we have been taught that purchasing things makes us happy. But the evidence is the opposite. Psychologist Martin Seligman has made the study of happiness his life's work. His work is outlined on the website Authentic Happiness.[15]

In a nutshell, there are three types of happiness:
- » Happiness based on pleasure and gratification
- » Happiness based on the embodiment of strengths
- » Happiness based on meaning and purpose

Of these, happiness based on pleasure and gratification is the shortest-lived happiness. So while buying things can make you happy, it doesn't

---

15 https://www.authentichappiness.sas.upenn.edu/

last. If we go back to the hierarchy of needs, once the basics are taken care of, we want and need:
- » Meaningful relationships
- » Self-esteem and accomplishment and
- » Self-actualisation through realising our potential.

Time and time again, some of the poorest communities in the world often hold some of the happiest people. That is because their community works together and supports each other through meaningful relationships. I'm not advocating for poverty, but I'm pointing out that happiness is rarely measured in material goods.

Many people think that winning the lottery will bring them happiness. Know what? Research on lottery winners worldwide suggests that a significant portion of them experience financial challenges or even bankruptcy within a few years of their win. Furthermore, studies have shown that winning the lottery does not necessarily make you happier or healthier.[16] Why? Because it's not about the money! It's about what is going on in your head around money and material things.

---

16 https://www.cnbc.com/2017/08/25/heres-why-lottery-winners-go-broke.html

Chapter 12

Understanding yourself

This is the best bit of all.

I have spent much time on money because it is the hardest part of the equation to master. Well done if you are now in charge of your finances and know where you are going with it all.

Becoming part of a community, whether as a renter or a buyer, is also a stage that is required for your mental and physical well-being. Again, you will be happier if that has been achieved or is underway.

Self-actualisation is the most ephemeral of the steps to be taken in the hierarchy we are following.

People will say to follow your passion. Well, duh. But many people don't have a passion. Passions are usually associated with the arts – passion for acting, music, singing, writing, whatever. You can have a passion for hunting or cars too. You can have a passion for anything. But what if you don't have any passions? I don't have any real passions, but I'm interested in many things individually. So how do we discover how to be the best person we can be and reach our fullest potential?

I don't have a complete answer for this, but I have a method I'm happy with that might help you get started.

You need to do a bit of naval gazing for this, and the guides are online questionnaires. You need to understand yourself better than you currently do, which is what these questionnaires are helpful for.

My first assessment tool is the Myers-Briggs test.

The Myers-Briggs Type Indicator was devised by mother and daughter psychologists to give insight into type theory that can be applied to groups and individuals. This would identify four basic preferences (from Jung's theory) and clarify the 16 resulting personality types that emerged from the preferences.[17]

So, this is how it works. There are four preferences:

Favourite world, information, decisions and structure.

- » Favourite world: Do you prefer to focus on the outer world or your inner world? This is called Extraversion (E) or Introversion (I).
- » Information: Do you prefer to focus on the essential information you take in, or do you like to interpret and add meaning? This is called Sensing (S) or Intuition (N).
- » Decisions: When making decisions, do you prefer to first look at logic and consistency or first look at the people and special circumstances? This is called Thinking (T) or Feeling (F).
- » Structure: In dealing with the outside world, do you prefer to get things decided or do you like to stay open to new information and options? This is called Judging (J) or Perceiving (P).

When you decide on your preference in each category, you have your personality type, which can be expressed as a code with four letters. It's not generally left to you to decide. A questionnaire determines the four preferences in your personality based on your answers.

The 16 personality types of the Myers-Briggs Type Indicator® instrument are listed here as they are often shown in what is called a 'type table'.

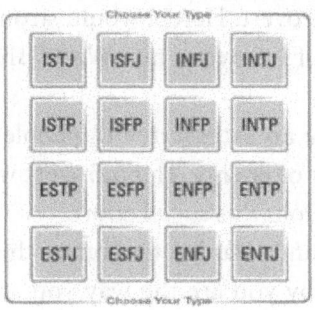

Choose Your Type

ISTJ	ISFJ	INFJ	INTJ
ISTP	ISFP	INFP	INTP
ESTP	ESFP	ENFP	ENTP
ESTJ	ESFJ	ENFJ	ENTJ

Choose Your Type

---

17 *Excerpted from the MBTI® Manual: A Guide to the Development and Use of the Myers-Briggs Type Indicator®* https://www.myersbriggs.org/

This is generally a workplace test to see if you have certain attributes for certain things, but it is also helpful as a 'know yourself' tool. It can provide insights into the type of gifts that you uniquely have and how best to apply them. At the end of doing this test, you will be categorised into a four-letter 'type'. In total, there are 16 combinations of these letters possible. None of these types is better than the other. They just are.

Each four-letter combination comes with a full explanation of what they mean.

This isn't carved in stone. These are just indicators to provide insight into why certain situations are uncomfortable or why you are particularly good in some situations and not others. So, it's a good one.

You can do it here: https://www.mbtionline.com/

I am INTP. I am introvert, intuitive, thinking and perceptive. For instance, I knew I hated getting into verbal sparring matches, but now I know that is because I am introverted. I'm never going to win a verbal sparring match with an extrovert (and they are just the sort of people who love them!). So I now avoid those situations and allow myself to respond in my own time. This has removed a tremendous amount of stress from my life. In any verbal confrontation, I turn away and respond with a written reply later.

It doesn't just highlight things like that. For instance, many people challenge the description of me as an introvert as socially, I am often at the centre of things. But this is where you need to understand the nature of being an introvert. Here, I would strongly suggest a reading of Quiet: The Power of Introverts in a World That Can't Stop Talking by Susan Cain.

You can seem to be an extrovert with people you know very well, but this will take a lot of energy. The introvert will need quality quiet time later to recover from this social effort.

While it may sound wanky to some, this insight gives you information about why you are the way you are. And why you feel the way you feel sometimes. It's important information. How can we ever expect anyone else to understand us if we don't understand ourselves? And this is what we want the most, isn't it? To be loved and understood?

My next best survey to take is the Signature Strengths Survey on the Authentic Happiness site. You will have to create a free account. Then look for the VIA Survey of Character Strengths questionnaire. This will guide you into the strengths that drive you and are important to you daily. This is also an important underlying driver of your happiness. One of my top five was authenticity. I once found myself in a job where I was being asked to do things I thought were wrong. Even though I needed the money, I resigned. You might think that seems self-evident, but it's not. You will be miserable if you need authenticity and are in a false environment that doesn't jibe with your values. That goes for all the values listed, no matter which are yours.

This survey blew me away. Once I knew my top five strengths, I set about getting them into my life every day. Another one of those signature strengths in my survey was fun. I had to be having some fun in my day. Even if those things were not available in my workplace, I could ensure I found them some other way throughout my day. And I did, by volunteering with a great group of gardeners and then taking up line dancing. (I know!) Laugh? OMG!

It also meant that when I decided I needed to look for a new sort of work, I at least had an inkling of the kind of environment that would make me happy. Having fun was just one item on the list. If I could find a job or an environment that would allow me to experience, say, three of the signature strengths I value, it would be a perfect environment for me.

This is what self-actualising is about. Discover your strengths, explore your values, ethics and beliefs and test them. Push against what you were told and work out what you think. It has an incredible effect on your daily life and outlook. It's super empowering.

The VIA Character strengths survey will highlight the bottom five strengths (weaknesses needing work). This was also hugely enlightening. The site then goes on to give ideas on how to do that. One of my weaknesses was a lack of gratitude. I work on that every day.

You can do many surveys with Authentic Happiness, but this was the one that changed my insight into the person I was and what I needed in my day-to-day life to be happy.

If you're interested, Professor Martin Seligman has several books on the topic and much newer work since.

This can help you on your way to self-actualisation. I also use CALM, a subscription meditation app that provides guided meditations. It's remarkable the difference a 10-minute meditation can make to your mental attitude. It allows a bit of quiet reflection in a hurly-burly, hectic world.

How else do you self-actualise? Garden, crafts, music, woodwork, read, play, exercise, volunteer, learn a language, go back to school, explore ideas, travel, teach, sing, hike, try something new, go back to something you enjoyed as a child.

The real test of something that enriches your life is finding flow. Flow is when you do not notice the time passing while you are doing it. Flow is losing yourself in your activity and not being distracted for hours at a time. Take time for the you that you always wanted to be. We are ongoing works of art. We are never finished.

Imagine yourself in five years, 10 years and more into the future. What does it look like? Who are you with? What are you doing? Spend some time visualizing this world and set goals around it. I'm not an advocate for the universe sending you what you want, but if you know what you want, it is much easier to achieve it. Use your brain to make the vision become reality as a goal set in stone.

Conclusion

Financial freedom and fulfillment

Are we there yet?

Let's review. If you have been following along, the blue line on your money graph is going up (increased income, side hustle, savings) and your red line is going down (monthly outgoings, fewer bills, less shopping, fewer unpleasant surprises).

Your savings are increasing, earning meaningful interest by being invested in safe stocks. Never let money sit. Make it work.

You are living in a modest home that meets your needs. You are not heating, cooling and furnishing rooms used for 15 minutes a week. Less space means less money to maintain and fewer items to curate.

You have only what you need. You aren't storing heaps of crap that you can't or won't use in your lifetime. Clear the decks and send them to a place where they will be used by someone who needs them.

To put this sort of minimalist thinking into perspective, I bought and read a book called Goodbye Things by Fumio Sasaki. It is an engaging read, and I followed through on many of his suggestions. But when he advocated getting rid of the bed and sleeping on the floor, my old bones arced up. No chance of that!

Another excellent read for a fresh perspective on work is a book by one of the early digital pioneers, Tim Ferriss, called The 4-Hour Workweek. It focuses on examining how we can change our lives to working to live rather than living to work. Very much the sort of thing I'm trying to encourage here, but differently.

Rent rather than buy items like boats, jet skis and trailers that are not used regularly. These things BURN money and need space. Space costs more money.

You have enough clothes, but not closets full. You have good quality but no $900 t-shirts. No kidding. I heard this was a thing. Use your head. Just because someone wants to charge you doesn't mean it's worth it.

You are in your neighbourhood and you know that people care about you and that you care about them.

When you purchase, you are aware of the spend, where it was made and by whom out of what. You manage your carbon footprint by minimising it.

You contribute. You have found meaningful work. You are working on your self-development as well as encouraging others. You are calm. You are secure. You have a plan. You have choices.

Congratulations. That is Maslow's hierarchy realised.

Resources

These are some of the resources used or referred to in this book.
- Your Money or Your Life by Vicki Robin and Joe Dominguez

Money-saving websites:
- Frugal and Thriving (Australia-based) https://www.frugalandthriving.com.au
- Clever Girl Finance (USA-based) https://www.clevergirlfinance.com
- Zero Waste Home https://zerowastehome.com
- Honest to Goodness https://www.goodness.com.au
- Australian Bureau of Statistics https://www.abs.gov.au/statistics/people/people-and-communities/gender-indicators-australia/nov-2019#economic-security
- MoneySmart https://moneysmart.gov.au
- SmartCompany smartcompany.com.au
- Australian National Debt Helpline: 1800 007 007
- One Big Switch https://onebigswitch.com.au
- Imperfect Foods https://imperfect-foods.medium.com
- How to Tell Whether Expired Food is Safe to Eat https://www.consumerreports.org/food-safety/how-to-tell-whether-expired-food-is-safe-to-eat-a1083080425/
- Earth911 https://earth911.com/living-well-being/50-diy-natural-handmade-beauty-products-that-make-great-gifts/
- Workplace Gender Equality Agency https://www.wgea.gov.au

- » Fair Work Commission awarded aged care workers an interim 15% wage increase in November 2022: https://ministers.dewr.gov.au/burke/fair-work-decision-aged-care
- » Plan International https://plan-international.org/publications/the-state-of-the-worlds-girls-2009-girls-in-the-global-economy/
- » Tracking Happiness https://www.trackinghappiness.com/how-to-want-less/
- » Positive Psychology https://positivepsychology.com/happiness/
- » Consumerism and Well-Being in India and the UK: Identity Projection and Emotion Regulation as Underlying Psychological Processes https://link.springer.com/article/10.1007/s12646-011-0065-2
- » Dress for Success https://dressforsuccess.org/
- » Lost super: https://www.ato.gov.au/forms/searching-for-lost-super/
- » Extra Home Loan Repayments Calculator https://www.canstar.com.au/calculators/extra-home-loan-repayments-calculator/
- » Overconsumption Makes Us Unhappy https://www.psychologytoday.com/au/blog/buddhist-economics/201803/why-over-consumption-is-making-us-unhappy
- » Authentic Happiness https://www.authentichappiness.sas.upenn.edu
- » Myers-Briggs test: https://www.mbtionline.com

Author's Biography

Judy Williams worked for forty years in the television industry in Canada and Australia. A large part of her career was in news and current affairs, leading to an executive position with the Australian Broadcasting Corporation.

This book is based on her experience of becoming financially independent after a great deal of money mayhem in her marriage.

Judy is retired and lives near her sons and grandchildren in the Hunter Valley, New South Wales, Australia.

Shawline Publishing Group Pty Ltd
www.shawlinepublishing.com.au

**SHAWLINE
PUBLISHING
GROUP**